FOCUS GROUPS IN
SOCIAL RESEARCH

INTRODUCING QUALITATIVE METHODS provides a series of volumes which introduce qualitative research to the student and beginning researcher. The approach is interdisciplinary and international. A distinctive feature of these volumes is the helpful student exercises.

One stream of the series provides texts on the key methodologies used in qualitative research. The other stream contains books on qualitative research for different disciplines or occupations. Both streams cover the basic literature in a clear and accessible style, but also cover the 'cutting edge' issues in the area.

FOCUS GROUPS IN SOCIAL RESEARCH

Michael Bloor
Jane Frankland
Michelle Thomas
Kate Robson

SAGE Publications
London • Thousand Oaks • New Delhi

First published 2001

Reprinted 2002

SAGE Publications Ltd
6 Bonhill Street
London EC2A 4PU

SAGE Publications Inc
2455 Teller Road
Thousand Oaks, California 91320

SAGE Publications India Pvt Ltd
32, M-Block Market
Greater Kailash – I
New Delhi 110 048

British Library Cataloguing in Publication data

A catalogue record for this book is available
from the British Library

ISBN 0 7619 5742 1
ISBN 0 7619 5743 X (pbk)

Library of Congress catalog record available

Typeset by Mayhew Typesetting, Rhayader, Powys
Printed and bound in Great Britain by Biddles Ltd., Guildford and King's Lynn

Contents

Preface

This book is intended as a standard or supplementary text for students and as a guide to practicing social researchers. It is aimed at undergraduates taking research methods courses, and those taking the growing number of postgraduate research methods courses and professional post-qualifying courses in areas such as medicine, social work, education and nursing. Although the first academic publications on focus group methods appeared in the 1940s, their modern use in academic social research has grown out of their usage in commercial market research, where focus groups first began to be widely used in the 1960s. However, focus group practice in academic social research has now diverged quite markedly from practice in commercial market research and a modern text which tried to cover both types of research practice would end up irremediably confused. So this book specifically covers focus group practice in academic social research. Like all the books in Sage's 'Introducing Qualitative Methods' series, our aim has been to produce a nuts and bolts text, emphasizing the practical tasks of design, composition, conduct and analysis, using illustrative examples and suggesting practice exercises. Naturally, and we hope pardonably, we have drawn extensively on our own experiences of past focus group research projects.

The plan of the book is straightforward. The first chapter traces the origins of modern focus group research and considers both the kinds of research topics which focus groups are best able to address as a standalone method and the rather larger role for focus groups as part of a multi-method research design. Chapter 2 is concerned with how focus groups are composed – issues of recruitment, numbers of participants and numbers of groups; in particular, this chapter addresses the debate about whether or not focus groups should be drawn from pre-existing social groups. Chapter 3 deals with the planning and conduct of the groups – the choice of venues, the use of pre-group questionnaires and debriefings, audio recording, facilitation (including the avoidance of painful silences), ideal length and conventions of payment. We deal at particular length with the design of focusing exercises to assist the discussion and ease inter-group comparisons. We aim to combat the belief that the conduct of successful focus groups is some esoteric, incommunicable, craft skill found only among a small coterie of experienced, highly sensitized and extraordinarily sociable specialist research consultants. In fact, of course, successful focus groups are mainly a matter of forward planning. Focus groups, real and virtual, generate large amounts of very rich data, so Chapter 4 is concerned with the transcription, indexing and systematic analysis of focus group data. Chapter 5 concerns the new possibilities for focus group practice found in computer-mediated communications: 'virtual' focus groups have a number of advantages over 'real life' focus groups and are likely to be increasingly popular. We give particular attention to the ways of setting up these online discussion fora, with moderated, closed, distribution lists being preferable for most purposes. Chapter 6, the concluding chapter, summarizes the earlier chapters as a set of ground rules (a rough guide only, not a template) for the use and deployment of focus groups and ends with a discussion of how far focus groups can assist in public participation in the research process.

We wish to acknowledge the help of David Silverman, editor of the 'Introducing Qualitative Methods' series and the help of, successively, Miranda Nunhofer and Beth Crockett at Sage. We would also like to thank Lesley Pugsley for allowing us to draw on material from her focus group work in schools.

1

Trends and uses of focus groups

CONTENTS

Beginnings

A cherished didactic method in the academy is that of beginning the study of every topic with a brisk canter through the founding fathers and occasional founding mothers. It is a method that has its apogee in the notorious Oxford University English curriculum that bewildered and bored generations of students with studies of Anglo-Saxon (taught by the inventor of Bilbo Baggins and Hobbitry, Prof. J.R.R. Tolkien). Sociology departments have tried to follow the same path, and even courses that end (appropriately) with postmodernism may start by attempting an exegesis of wordy antediluvians like Herbert Spencer. The Founding Father Method has several advantages for the academic: it demonstrates an impressive breadth (if not depth) of learning; it economizes on the need for originality in one's own thinking by lengthy recapitulation of the thoughts of others; and it elevates one's own puny thoughts by emphasizing their continuity with the hallowed precepts of The Past.

So, to begin at The Beginning, focus groups as a research method originated in the work of the Bureau of Applied Social Research at Columbia University in the 1940s. Under the leadership of Paul Lazarsfeld, the Columbia bureau was conducting commercial market research on audience responses to radio soap operas and the like. The arrival of Robert Merton at Columbia coincided with Lazarsfeld receiving a government contract (from the delightfully named Office of Facts and Figures) to assess audience responses to the government's own wartime radio propaganda programmes and Lazarsfeld invited Merton to work with him on the project. By Merton's own account (Merton, 1987), he found an established experimental procedure in operation: groups of approximately 12 people at a time would be seated in the radio studio and each chair would have a red and a green button at the side; members of the group were asked to press the red button each time they responded negatively to what they heard and to press the green button when they felt positive about something. Dissatisfied with an approach which simply quantified positive and negative responses, Merton set about developing an *interviewing procedure* for the groups, which would help researchers to describe the subjective reactions of the group members to the programmes they heard. Over a series of audience studies (involving print and film audiences as well as radio), researchers at the bureau (not just Merton, but also Alberta Curtis, Marjorie Fiske, Patricia Kendall and others) evolved a fairly standardized set of procedures for these interviews. These procedures were summarized in Merton and Kendall's (1946) article for the *American Journal of Sociology*, 'The focused interview'. In 1956, Merton, Fiske and Kendall collaborated on a book with the same title.

The works of founding fathers in sociology are rarely 'A good read', witness the collected works of Vilfredo Pareto. But the Merton and Kendall paper still repays study. For example, their apt description of the mental state they sought to inculcate in their research subjects during the interview: they termed this state 'retrospective introspection' (Merton and Kendall, 1946: 550). Or again, their emphasis on the importance in analysing their group data of concentrating on discrepancies ('deviant cases') in reports between different groups (Merton and Kendall, 1946: 542–544): an analytic procedure more commonly referred to as 'analytic induction', following Znaniecki (1968).

Good read or not, the Merton and Kendall paper passed into a degree of obscurity. The interviewing procedures developed at Columbia became part and parcel of the methodology of the *individual* depth or qualitative interview and academic sociologists rarely conducted group interviews. However, the Columbia bureau had started out doing audience research for commercial radio and the *commercial* potential of focus groups to marketing organizations and advertisers remained. Small wonder that focus groups should resurface as a commercial market research technique in the 1960s. Greenbaum of Groups Plus, who was conducting focus groups as a market researcher in American living rooms in the early 1970s, finds no continuity with the earlier Columbia studies:

Focus groups have been commonly used in market research since the late 1960s, although some packaged food marketing organizations used the technique as early as the late 1950s, and some people even trace the beginning of the focus group technique back to publication in 1941 [sic] of The Focused Interview by Robert K. Merton, Marjorie Fiske and Patricia Kendall. Most research practitioners agree, however, that the technique began to be used regularly only in the late 1960s and early 1970s and that it has grown in popularity every year since. (Greenbaum, 1998: 167)

Tom Greenbaum and market research focus groups have both come a long way since those early days of the Proctor & Gamble Charmin Toilet Tissue campaign (Greenbaum, 1998: xv). Greenbaum quotes estimates that more than a 1,000 Americans earn the bulk of their livelihoods conducting focus groups and the average full-time focus group moderator conducts over 100 groups per year. This considerable industry has its own literature – trade magazines, websites and books (Greenbaum's among them) – and it is not our intention to contribute to that large literature with this small book. Instead, we wish to address those academic researchers who are seeking to *adapt* commercial focus group practice to academic research needs.

The evident success of focus groups as a marketing tool in the private sector eventually led public sector organizations to use focus groups for their own marketing purposes – to assess the impact of health education campaigns, for example. Often this public sector research was contracted to private sector marketing organizations with previous experience of focus group work for the private sector and, of course, the techniques used in these early public sector studies were the same as those in the private sector. Even where the public sector organizations chose to do the focus group work 'in house' in their own research departments, the techniques used were initially those of the private sector because no other models of practice were available. However, this parallelism of public sector and private sector practice has not been maintained.

The divergence of public sector and private sector focus group work has two sources. First, the requirement to keep costs competitive has led private sector researchers to adopt, as standard, practices which compromised between economy and quality. This is not to say, of course, that the private sector has failed on quality: self-evidently, this booming industry has delivered value for money – it could hardly be so successful otherwise. Additionally, where quality of data, depth of analysis and rigour of comparison were considerations for the client that outranked economy, then of course it was always an option for the client to make this clear in the contract and for the contractor to modify practice and price accordingly. Although not all clients would perhaps have appreciated that they had this option. The compromise between economy and quality can be seen most clearly in respect of the *analysis* of focus group data. Krueger (1994: 143–144) identifies four possible analysis strategies: transcript-based analysis, the most rigorous; tape-based analysis, based on careful listening to the tapes but not on the study of transcripts; note-based analysis; and memory-based analysis. However, standard practice for private contractors to the UK public sector has involved a mix of the last two strategies, with group facilitators/moderators using their notes as background for an oral debriefing to a report writer, who in turn will collate the efforts of several facilitators (perhaps working in different parts of the country) in his/her report to the client; audio recordings of the groups may be made, but used sparingly, and mainly as a check that the contracted-for groups have indeed been run as contracted. There is no need to dwell on the loss of understanding of group interaction involved in the double selectivity of recall of first the facilitator and then the report writer.

A second reason for the divergence of public sector focus group practice from that of the private sector has lain in the realization that focus groups can be used for more than the mere assessment of group reactions to stimuli. It is this issue of the extended uses of focus groups to which we turn now.

Access to group meanings, processes and norms

Focus groups can be used for more than, say, the generation of information on collective views on what is the optimum sized gap between the top of the soap powder packet and the level of soap powder inside, or on whether or not groups react positively to pictures of a prematurely bald UK politician wearing a baseball cap. Focus groups can yield data on the *meanings* that lie behind those group assessments – do groups perhaps believe that manufacturers are trying to misrepresent the amount of soap powder they are offering the consumer when a large empty space is found in the top of a newly opened packet? Similarly, focus groups can yield data on the uncertainties, ambiguities, and *group processes* that lead to and underlie group assessments – is the politician's baseball cap indicative of an unseemly sensitivity towards one's baldness and unbecoming vanity about one's appearance? or is it a praiseworthy attempt to signal one's solidarity with the concerns of younger people? but if the latter, isn't it the case that any UK citizen over 25 wearing a baseball cap looks like a complete prat? and doesn't the politician's failure to realize this demonstrate that he is therefore completely out of touch with young people? Relatedly, focus groups can also throw light on the *normative understandings* that groups draw upon to reach their collective judgements – manufacturers are expected to attempt to mislead consumers and no older person can successfully pass themselves off for any length of time as 'A young person'. It is the access that focus groups are said to provide to these group meanings, processes and norms that accounts for much of the interest currently being shown by academic researchers.

Even late-modern societies remain normatively ordered; norms of conduct remain the mainsprings of human action. Of course, late modern societies are characterized by agency and choice, where people (all but the considerable minority of the most disadvantaged) can reflexively construct their identities and motives, mixing and matching from a diverse range of materials and be influenced by diverse groups and sources (Giddens, 1991). Relatedly, many of the principal sources of normative influence of 50 years ago (such as the workgroup and the neighbourhood) have lost much of their determining force, undermined by technical and economic changes and cross-cut by new sources of influence from soccer to soap operas. Moreover, individuals choose their own affiliations, constructing their own selves in the process, perhaps literally like groups of bodybuilders, or playfully like Klingon-speaking Trekkies. Nevertheless, human behaviour is still normative, all that has changed is that the sources of normative influence are more diverse, complex and interactive; our selves are reflexive constructs, but they are very much more likely to be collective than individual constructs; choice does not equate with freedom. It is precisely because behaviour remains normative, but is more subtly and variously influenced than the past, that interest has grown in research methods like focus groups which can access the rich texture of these influences.

In everyday life, the normative order underlying behaviours and opinions is rarely articulated. It is part of our taken for granted stock of knowledge (Schutz, 1964a; Schutz and Luckmann, 1974); it only has that degree of clarity and determinacy required for the conduct of everyday activities; and it is assumed to be shared by our associates (family, friends, workmates) until experience proves otherwise. The circumstances under which we are led to examine, elaborate and assess our normative assumptions are unusual – Schutz instances the estrangement of the war veteran returning to his old job as a cigar clerk (Schutz, 1964b) – under normal circumstances and in normal interaction we only refer to those normative assumptions briefly, allusively and in passing. There is no need to spell them out in more detail: we assume their rectitude and assume others share our views. Indeed, the ability to recognize these allusions (the 'indexical expressions' of ethnomethodology (Garfinkel, 1967)) is the hallmark of the competent collectivity member. And the very force of these normative influences on the collectivity may lie partly in their unexamined character (Bourdieu, 1977). It follows therefore that these normative assumptions are only slowly and progressively revealed to the ethnographer immersing her/himself in a collectivity, and even then (being alluded to, instead of articulated) they are largely inductively elaborated rather than directly recorded.

The situation of the focus group, in principle and with a fair wind, can provide the occasion and the stimulus for collectivity members to articulate those normally unarticulated normative assumptions. The group is a socially legitimated occasion for participants to engage in

'retrospective introspection', to attempt collectively to tease out previously taken for granted assumptions. This teasing out may only be
partial (with many areas of ambiguity or opacity remaining) and it may
be disputatious (as limits are encountered to shared meanings), but it
may yield up as much rich data on group norms as long periods of
ethnographic fieldwork. There are a number of problems with focus
group data (problems we will examine in detail in subsequent chapters)
and there are many possible objectives of sociological data collection in
addition to that of gathering data on group norms. But in respect of that
one limited objective – the study of group norms – focus groups should
be the sociological method of choice, providing concentrated and
detailed information on an area of group life which is only occasionally,
briefly and allusively available to the ethnographer over months and
years of fieldwork.

The ambiguity of group norms revealed by focus group analysis is a
characteristic structural feature of any normative order. As early ethnomethodological studies by Garfinkel and his followers convincingly
demonstrated (Coulter, 1974; Zimmerman and Wieder, 1971), all rules
are essentially contingent and defeasible in the sense that any competent
collectivity member is able in principle to elaborate on the sense of the
rule to justify their current behaviour, or to specify the limits of the rule's
application in order to excuse current behaviour as not breaching the
rule. The same ethnomethodological studies did not, of course, destroy
the warrant for seeing social behaviour as rule-governed, because norms
may be *essentially* contingent and defeasible while remaining *practically*
fixed and constraining under normal circumstances. This is because most
collectivity members under most circumstances are not motivated to
elaborate on stable formulations of rules: these stable formulations of
rules become familiar, routinized and invested with reverence; and
they may only be renegotiated or elaborated with superordinates or
intimates at some cost to the individual (Bloor, 1980). However, the focus
group process not only lays bare the rule, it also makes apparent
(to facilitator and group members alike) that its stability is illusory, that
the rule in question is essentially contingent and defeasible: the very
process of the focus group itself (inviting group members to inspect,
elaborate upon, and question rules that we normally take for granted)
calls forth and demonstrates the intrinsically ambiguous character of
group norms. So focus groups are simultaneously the best method for
accessing group norms and also the best method for demonstrating that
the group norms thus elicited cannot be unproblematically applied in
organizational decision-making or public policy. One of the challenges
for focus group researchers (which we revisit later in this book) is to find
ways of incorporating focus group methods into participative public
decision-making, rather than having the focus group findings treated
simply as a resource in expert deliberations (Cunningham-Burley et al.,
1999; Johnson, 1996). But even as a resource for expert deliberations, the

ambiguous character of group norms derived from focus groups does not allow their unproblematic utilization by experts.

The application of any group norm in any given setting requires a prior act of interpretation, requires the attribution of meaning. Such interpretations are only rarely unique to the individual, more commonly they are shared with others in the individual's social groups, part of a common stock of knowledge. This common stock of knowledge is the basis of social action, since recipes for action are tied to given interpretations of the situation, but the various elements of this stock of knowledge are not always clear and distinct. Interpretations have only that degree of clarity required for the person's purpose at hand: if that purpose changes (if, say, an initial interpretation is questioned), then the interpretation may be further elaborated, different and competing interpretations may be considered, and the appropriateness of the initial recipe for action may be now thought problematic (Schutz, 1962; 1970). It therefore follows that the discussions occurring within focus groups will provide rich data on the *group meanings* associated with a given issue. But the very act of making such group meanings a topic of group discussion will lay bare the provisional character of such interpretations. Just as focus group data on norms may demonstrate the essential ambiguity of norms, so focus group data on meanings may demonstrate the essential ambivalence of interpretations: the rather chaotic character of the findings is not a defect of the method, it is a faithful reflection of the subject matter.

The group meanings accessed in focus group discussions are, of course, expressed in the argot and everyday language of the group, not translated into the terminology of the researcher. Since the researcher is present simply to facilitate the discussion, then ideally the group participants should be addressing each other and therefore using group terms and group categories, so-called 'indigenous coding systems' (Holstein and Gubrium, 1995). The focus group may therefore give the researcher privileged access to in-group conversations which contain 'indigenous' terms and categories in the situations of their use.

The same focus group discussions also reflect internal group processes and formal and informal group structures. Meetings of the Society of Friends (the Quakers) are formally democratic and unstructured, with no minister to lead the meeting and with all members waiting quietly for one of their number to be inspired to say something. But it is said that 100 years ago meetings in the York Meeting House found York Quakers routinely deferring to members of the Rowntree (chocolate) family, whose social and economic prominence in the town meant that they always spoke first in the meetings. Similarly, in focus groups formed from a pre-existing social group, some of the processes of the pre-existing group may be captured within the focus group. So, for example, a focus group being conducted with a pre-existing workgroup may reflect the hierarchical relationships within that workgroup: a focus group conducted in a health centre team meeting may find, for example, the nurses in the team deferring to the general practitioners. Likewise, mixed sex groups of adolescents may capture within the group process broader patterns of boy–girl interaction. It may be possible to address such differences in the planning and composition of focus groups: for example, by holding separate girl and boy groups as well as mixed sex groups, or by holding a group composed of nurses from several different health centres, so that differences in group processes between differently composed groups may be highlighted.

Of course, there are difficulties of execution and (as we shall see) not all focus groups succeed in their research objectives. Nevertheless, it is clear that the access that focus groups allow to group norms, group meanings and group processes makes them, in principle, a useful research method in their own right alongside surveys, depth interviews and ethnography. However, more common than the use of focus groups as a stand-alone method, is the use of focus groups as an adjunct of other methods.

Focus groups as an adjunct to other methods

As we have seen, the current academic interest in focus groups as a main or stand-alone method of data collection is contemporary, not historical. It is possible to pick out early pioneering studies which centred on focus group methods, but they only have prominence with the 20/20 vision of hindsight: in *their* day, they were swamped by other studies using other methods, pre-eminently survey methods. And using foresight rather than hindsight, it seems quite plausible that there will only be a rather limited future role for focus groups as a main source of data in academic research, since they are superior to other methods only for the study of group norms and group understandings, and even here their superiority to ethnographic study is partly the superiority of convenience or accessibility (ethnographic work being difficult to undertake in increasingly private late-modern societies). When it comes to documenting behaviour, focus groups are less suitable than individual interviews: there is an understandable tendency for atypical behaviours to be unreported or under-reported in group settings. When one of the tasks of focus groups is to arrive at a group consensus on a given topic, it is to be expected that deviant experiences will be silenced. Focus groups, particularly virtual focus groups, do have an academic research future as a main method of data collection, but their role will be a circumscribed one while the main task of sociology remains the mapping of behaviour and behaviour change.

However, focus groups have a much larger part to play as an ancillary method, alongside and complementing other methods. We can note the following ancillary roles for focus groups: first, their use in pre-pilot work, to provide a contextual basis for survey design; second, their use as a contemporary extension of survey and other methods, to provide an interpretative aid to survey findings; and third, their use as a method of communicating findings to research subjects, to provide a means of discharging fieldwork obligations while simultaneously generating new insights on the early findings. As an ancillary method, therefore, focus groups may operate at the beginning, middle and end of projects.

Pre-pilot focus groups

Pre-pilot focus groups may be used as an alternative to depth interviews in the initial phase of a large survey study. Prior to the drafting and piloting of the survey instrument itself, focus groups may be used in the early days of the study for exploratory purposes, to inform the development of the later stages of the study. This exploration will typically be wide-ranging (because the focus group, like the wind, bloweth where it listeth) but may concentrate on certain priority topics, on generating contextual data (illustrative stories and cautionary tales), or on everyday group language (vernacular terms, indexical expressions and indigenous coding categories).

Using focus groups for preliminary exploration of certain topic areas is obviously most useful in those fields where survey planning is most difficult because relatively little is known (Vaughn et al., 1996), where prior research is lacking, or where deviant groups have knowledge concealed from others. For example, adolescents (everyone's favourite deviant group) in each generation develop, enforce and conceal new norms of group behaviour. Frankland's exploratory focus groups with South Wales secondary school pupils (Frankland and Bloor, 1999) were part of an evaluation of a schools-based smoking intervention which aimed to train popular pupils to intervene effectively with their peers to discourage smoking (Bloor et al., 1999). Of course, adolescent smoking behaviour has been a popular topic of health promotion research for many years, but adolescent peer groups may shift radically in their preoccupations and influences over time, and there are suggestions of such shifts in pupils' peer group norms in respect of smoking behaviour: the UK is one of several countries where the prevalence of smoking among pupils has been increasing in the 1990s, while adult smoking prevalences are falling (Diamond and Goddard, 1995). It was therefore only prudent, before piloting a survey instrument seeking to monitor changes over time in peer influences on pupils' smoking, to collect focus group data on how peer pressures to take up or quit smoking were *discussed* among pupils, on group discourses about peer pressures. Frankland conducted 12 groups with pupils in Years 8 and 9 (12 to 14 year-olds) from four secondary schools, with some single sex groups and some mixed groups and some groups deliberately including numbers of self-reported regular smokers or experimental smokers (Frankland and Bloor, 1999). Among other findings, Frankland found her groups would qualify the supposed peer pressures on ex-smokers to resume smoking: whether or not ex-smokers would suffer social exclusion depended on whether the friendship group was one of 'real friends' or one composed of people who 'use you for fags' (that is, sustain their smoking habit by smoking other people's cigarettes), highlighting the adolescent perception of the essentially collective character of adolescent smoking behaviour, that most early smoking and smoking experimentation takes place in group settings. Such findings can feed not just into survey designs, but also into the design of health promotion interventions. However, for such exploratory focus groups to realize their full potential as an ancillary method, it is necessary to time-schedule into the study design sufficient opportunity for a full analysis of the data. Too often, the period allocated for pre-pilot work in survey studies is insufficient to do more than run a few focus groups and gain the barest preliminary impression of the resultant transcript data.

The ancillary use of focus groups to generate contextual data is to be found in Barbour's (1999) use of such group data to develop vignettes for use in a subsequent survey. Vignettes are detailed hypothetical cases or scenarios in which respondents are invited to choose the correct interpretation or the likeliest course of action (West, 1982) and are a frequent component of contemporary surveys. For example, a recent WHO/MRC survey of HIV-related risk behaviour among drug injectors included vignettes of different social situations where injectors might be pressed into sharing their injecting equipment (McKeganey, 1995). The storytelling that is a natural component of all focus group discussions can be a rich source for constructing both the descriptive background of the vignette and the alternative courses of action. Focus group data may thus provide a resource for survey designers which enables them to contextualize at least some survey questions within the everyday reported experiences of respondents.

Relatedly, focus groups can be used to access the everyday language of research subjects, either as a first step towards the compilation of a taxonomy of vernacular terms (for example, Mays et al.s' 1992 study of the sexual vocabulary of black gay men) or to ensure that the terms chosen for use in a subsequent survey are ones which are consistently understood by respondents. For example, is it better in a sexual survey to use neutral terms like 'sexual intercourse' or slang terms? if the former, will all respondents understand the neutral term to refer to the same sexual practices? (does the term 'sexual intercourse' refer just to vaginal penetration by the penis? or also to anal penetration? also to oral sex? does it include withdrawal prior to ejaculation? and so on). If slang terms are used will all respondents understand all the slang? and will some respondents be embarrassed or offended by the use in the survey of slang terms? These issues can be explored by individual depth interviews or by focus groups, with the superiority of one exploratory method over another being unclear.

Focus groups within the main study or as aid to interpretation

Focus groups may also be used to interpret survey results, to provide meaning to reports of attitudes or behaviour. An instance of such meaning attribution is provided by the focus groups run by Kitzinger and her colleagues on audience responses to media messages on HIV/AIDS (Kitzinger, 1994a). Earlier surveys on people's understanding of HIV transmission routes had indicated that some respondents believed that donating blood was a behaviour that carried risks of HIV transmission, a finding that was viewed with alarm by the Scottish Blood Transfusion Service, for example, which feared a diminution in donations as a result. Indeed, in self-completion pre-focus group questionnaires, 4 per cent of Kitzinger and her colleagues' focus group participants reported that 'people who give blood at a blood donor centre were greatly or quite a lot at risk from AIDS'. The results of the focus group work, in contrast, showed that group members had no fears of infection from giving blood: the earlier survey data had failed to take into account that respondents did not necessarily distinguish in everyday speech between 'donating' and 'receiving' blood, any more than many of the population distinguish in their everyday speech between the verbs 'to lend' and 'to borrow'. Survey respondents, it now appeared, had recognized HIV could be transmitted in donated blood (prior to the introduction of heat-treated donations) and so indicated in their survey responses that blood donation was a risk for HIV, while remaining quite happy to give blood. Focus group data revealed that fears of a reduction in donations were unfounded, by attention to the meanings that underlay survey responses (Kitzinger, 1994a).

Relatedly, focus group data may be used in an adversarial way, to contest or qualify earlier survey data. Thus Waterton and Wynne (1999) used data from a series of focus groups in West Cumbria to contest the claims by Nirex UK that residents in the vicinity of the Sellafield nuclear site were supporters of the industry, claims made on the basis of opinion poll data at the time of the planning application to build a repository at Sellafield for low and intermediate level nuclear waste. The focus group data illustrate the provisional and developmental character of personal opinions, with group members qualifying and extending their views in the course of the discussion; these are aspects of attitudes which cannot be reflected in survey approaches. Additionally, opinion poll respondents have a 'reflexive capability' (Wynne, 1996), an ability to reflect on how the results of social research will be used and impact on their own lives, how in this case the results of the poll may impact on the local economy and job opportunities for themselves, their families and their neighbours; this reflexive capability (and its impact on opinion polls and focus groups alike) can also be revealed in group discussions. In sum, local residents' attitudes to the nuclear industry were altogether more complex, more qualified, more provisional and more reflexive than market research surveys could reveal. In one of those ironic situations so beloved of postmodernist writers, Wynne and his colleagues (themselves sociologists of science interested in the social role of scientific experts) champion focus groups as an alternative scientific technique to opinion polling and contest the conclusions drawn from earlier research – an adversarial contest between competing experts itself extensively analysed by other sociologists of science such as Jasanoff in her studies of scientific witnesses in the law courts (Jasanoff, 1995) and scientists on government advisory bodies (Jasanoff, 1990).

Alternatively, focus group work (past the pre-pilot stage) may be consciously built into a multi-method study design. The objective here may be primarily 'triangulation', that of using focus group data to compare with other data on the same topic gathered by other methods and of replicating the researcher's earlier findings. Or the objective may be primarily that of 'research participation', providing a forum for research subjects (now redesignated 'research participants') to play an active collaborative role in the research process. Needless to say, the objectives of triangulation and research participation are by no means mutually exclusive.

The use of focus groups for triangulation purposes does not rely on any special features of focus groups as a method, all that is required is that focus groups are a different method to that method with which they are being compared: for example, triangulation may be attempted by comparing results from structured interviews with those with depth interviews, or by comparing structured interviews with focus groups. Triangulation simply requires contrast: the corroboration of findings produced via one method by findings produced via another method, indicating that those findings are unlikely to be the result of measurement biases. Much of the growth in academic focus group research is probably owed to the parallel mushrooming commitment of academic researchers to triangulation. Particularly among qualitative researchers, grant proposals are increasingly likely to refer to multi-method triangulation as an emblem of the applicant's commitment to methodological rigour.

Like any buzzword, 'triangulation' is a term open to misuse ('grounded theory' is another). The term was popularized by the methods writer Norman Denzin in his book *The Research Act* (1989) and his own use of the term is somewhat ambiguous (see Bloor, 1997), allowing subsequent researchers who wished to do so to claim that triangulation is the social scientist's equivalent of the natural scientist's 'replication': triangulation was seen as a validation procedure, a procedure for replication *within* social settings in a similar manner to the natural scientist's replication *across* laboratory settings. This positivist view of triangulation is mendacious on two counts: first, it equates (wrongly) one method with another in respect of their suitability for addressing the research issue in question; and second, it assumes (wrongly) that the data produced by each method are directly comparable in respect of the order of specificity of their findings (Bloor, 1997). In fact, research methods are not readily substitutable: in any given research setting one particular method will be more suitable for the particular research topic than any other (this is, after all, why research texts are read). Why then should we reject the findings that are the product of a superior method simply because they have not been confirmed (triangulated) by an inferior method? And furthermore, research data generated by different methods will differ in their degree of contextualization: focus group data will contain highly specific anecdotes and stories which may serve to qualify or elaborate the general endorsement of a norm or an attitude found in responses to a structured questionnaire: direct comparison is not possible and neither is validation by triangulation.

Note however, that rejection of a validating role for triangulation should not be confounded with a rejection of multiple methods. Rather, analysis of different kinds of data (including focus group data) bearing on the same topic may serve to deepen and enrich a researcher's understanding of a topic. Extending the range of methods used may extend an initial analysis, but it is not a test of it. Running focus groups alongside other methods may act as an aid to interpretation (as in the HIV and blood donation example), but it is not a means of validation by triangulation. As multi-method approaches increase in popularity, as part of a commitment to methodological rigour, so the use of focus groups may increase, since there are only a finite number of different research methods which can be combined in a multi-methods design.

Focus groups and public participation

The issue of using focus groups, alongside other methods, to facilitate public participation in the research process, is one which merits extended treatment and is one we shall return to in the concluding chapter. Focus groups provide an ostensibly attractive medium for public participation in the research process: they are sociable events; they are time-limited; and they require no technical skills of the group members. They can of course be convened at any and several points in the research process: at the outset, to participate in decisions on the design and objectives of the study; over the main data-collection period to review progress and agree changes; and in the closing period to interpret findings, draw lessons and implement change.

There is, of course, a tension between laity and expertise. 'Well-informed citizens', to use a term from Schutz's (1964c) classic analysis of the social distribution of knowledge, believe they have the right and the capacity to weigh and choose between the different opinions of different experts, while experts will not accept lay persons as competent judges of their performances, submitting only to the judgements of their peers in the scientific 'core-set' (Collins, 1981). The political neutrality and dis-interestedness of science have come under increasing attack from both environmental activists and sociologists of science (see, for example, Jasanoff's 1995 study of the 'buying' of expert witnesses in the US court system). Citizens may accept social research as a public good and be willing to fund it through the public purse and act as respondents, but they may in turn demand the right to set research priorities, the right to regulate and oversee the conduct of research, and the right to debate the findings and their implications (see Tudor Hart's policy paper on public health research in the Valleys of South Wales, 'Going for Gold' (1999), as a recent example of such a social contractual claim). In principle, focus groups may appear a user-friendly method of allowing such public par-ticipation in social research. In practice, we should beware of deceptively simple technological fixes, and focus groups are no exception.

Where focus groups meet at the end of a project to consider the provisional findings (generated by other methods), then the deliberations of such focus groups have sometimes been considered to be a form of validation, 'member validation'. This can be defined as the use of one or more of an array of techniques (including focus groups) to demonstrate a supposed correspondence between the researcher's analysis and research participants' understandings of their social worlds (Emerson, 1981), the presentation of results to members and then asking 'if members recognize, understand and accept one's description' (Douglas, 1976: 131). Thus, in a series of ethnographic studies of different types of therapeutic communities (Bloor et al., 1988), Bloor wrote preliminary research reports and then facilitated focus group discussions with staff members about the findings.

The communities were not in most cases designed for long-term care and ex-patients/residents views could be more readily obtained by individual interview, but in one community Bloor was able to get together a group of ex-patients to discuss his report. The results (from both staff and ex-patient groups) were frequently gratifying: one group member talked about how reading the report was like catching sight of himself in a mirror, another talked about the report getting across the essence of certain things which he had 'never actually put into words before' (Bloor, 1997: 43). This kind of thing is meat and drink to a researcher coming to the end of a project, a seemingly clear demon-stration that the researcher has indeed understood and successfully reported members' social reality. But other reactions included a staff member who admitted that he had just skimmed through the report to read the fieldnote extracts in which he figured. Again, in another staff focus group, two members criticized the naivity of Bloor's report for its failure to acknowledge the psychodynamic concepts that underlay therapy in the community, but two years later (in a conversation over a drink in the pub) one of them stated that he had changed his mind about the report and he felt that the article Bloor had written (Bloor, 1981), based on the report, should be required reading for every new staff member. And further, another group member commended the reporting of what Bloor took to be a relatively minor aspect of the workings of the therapeutic community and ignored what Bloor took to be its central features. What is one to make of reactions like these? That members' judgements are provisional and subject to change, that members' judgements may be superficial and based on misperceptions, but most of all that to view end-of-study focus groups as a member validation exercise is to forget that focus groups are subject to methodological frailties in an analogous manner to the earlier (main) study methodology. Focus groups are not the authentic Voice of the People, they are simply one more social research method, problematized by difficulties in recruitment, conduct and analysis: they cannot be used to authenticate findings in the name of the public.

However, just as triangulating with focus groups is not scientific replication, but good research practice (insofar as multiple methods may extend and deepen an initial analysis), so using end-of-study focus groups to discuss initial findings is not validation, but it may be good research practice in three ways. First, as with triangulation, the end-of-study focus groups furnish additional data which provide a stimulus to qualify, deepen and extend the initial analysis. Second, running a focus group or series of focus groups for members who have been participants in the research is a convenient means of providing early feedback on the results to persons with no access to, or interest in, academic publications. And third, the promise of running such groups at the end of the project (and thus the promise that research participants will have early sight of, and the opportunity to comment on, findings) may well serve to facilitate access to some research settings. Even if early feedback were not thought to be a courtesy, it could be considered a strategic resource in access negotiations. In such early feedback focus groups, the initial research findings become the focusing exercise (see Chapter 3): the group may have had a pre-circulated synopsis of the findings, or the group may begin with a brief run-through of the results, then members may be asked to list the most important things with which they agreed in the report and to list the most important things with which they disagreed.

The same sociable and participative aspects of focus group research which have suggested the (erroneous) possibility of focus groups playing a validating role have also suggested to some the possibility that focus groups are an essentially feminist method, just as Oakley (1981), Finch (1984) and others have previously claimed that depth/qualitative interviews were an essentially feminist method. This is rather a dangerous and over-blown claim, just as the earlier claim about depth interviews was a dangerous and over-blown claim (see Reid's (1983) response to Oakley (1981), and Hammersley's (1995) overview of the debate). Focus group research generates rich data, but it does not access and report the 'voice of oppressed women' in some transparent and unmediated manner. Focus groups are fluid and not directly controlled by the researcher, but they may retain their own internal hierarchies (see, for example, Michell (1999) on status differences between participants in focus groups of teenage girls) and they need to be carefully facilitated if they are to generate comparable data. As Wilkinson (1999) has argued, focus groups are a useful research technique for the pursuit of feminist research topics, but they are not an *essentially* feminist method.

Relatedly, focus groups are sometimes presented as ideal environments for researching sensitive topics. Participants may feel more relaxed and less inhibited in the co-presence of friends and colleagues. And they may feel empowered and supported in the co-presence of those similarly situated to themselves. Particularly in the case of focus groups composed of pre-existing social groups, therefore, focus groups may be deemed to be the method of choice in researching certain sensitive topics. Once again, this is a potentially dangerous argument. Traditionally, social researchers addressing sensitive issues have attempted to provide maximum confidentiality and anonymity in an atmosphere of studied neutrality. Britain's first national survey of sexual behaviour, in many respects a model of good research practice, opted to conduct face-to-face interviews with respondents but the most 'sensitive' questions (on topics like numbers of different sexual partners) were contained within separate booklets to be self-completed and sealed by the respondent in the presence of the interviewer (Wellings et al., 1994). The issue here is not whether or not focus groups can prove an environment which permits frank discussion (undoubtedly they can), but rather whether such frank discussion in the presence of others is necessarily in the interests of the discussants. This is the issue of so-called 'over-disclosure' and is considered in more detail in Chapter 2. If focus groups are chosen as a suitable method for addressing a sensitive topic, then particular attention needs to be devoted to ensuring that participants suffer no harm as a result and the researcher would be wise to seek advice from a research ethics committee, if one is available. Participants may need to be reminded of the confidentiality and anonymity guarantees offered by the researcher and their own obligations to respect each other's wishes concerning confidentiality. Some individual participants may need an opportunity to review the experience of the group in individual 'debriefings' at the end of the group or as soon as practicable afterwards. Any attempts to treat the groups as a therapeutic experience should be vigorously discouraged: group psychotherapy needs a long specialist training.

Conclusion

The antecedents of focus groups *may* be traced back to the work of Merton and his colleagues at the Bureau of Applied Social Research at Columbia

University in the 1940s, but the contemporary interest in focus groups in academic research has really arisen out of the cross-over of the technique to academic social research from commercial market research, where it first became commonly used in America in the late-1960s. However, the academic research practice of focus groups has now diverged somewhat from that found in the commercial world, particularly in respect of analytic techniques where academic researchers increasingly rely on the systematic analysis of audiotranscripts (see Chapter 4).

This divergence between academic and commercial researchers has been generated by the realization of the former that focus groups can be used to collect data on more than just group reactions to stimuli: they can be used to generate data on the group meanings that lie behind such collective assessments, on the group processes that lead to such assessments, and on the normative understandings that groups draw upon to reach such assessments. Box 1.1 summarizes the advantages that focus groups have over other research methods. In late-modern societies where identity is reflexive but behaviour remains normative, albeit subject to a widening range of influences, focus groups provide a valuable resource for documenting the complex and varying processes through which group norms and meanings are shaped, elaborated and applied. In the access they provide to norms and meanings, focus groups are not just the time-pressed researcher's poor substitute for ethnographic fieldwork, they are a mainstream method to address those study topics in increasingly privatised societies which are less open to observational methods.

BOX 1.1   FOCUS GROUPS VERSUS OTHER METHODS

- Focus groups may provide an acceptable economical alternative to ethnography in generating data on group meanings, group processes of meaning generation, and (most importantly) group norms.
- Focus groups are not a good source of data on group behaviour or attitudes, since intra-group variations will be under-reported. They are therefore rarely an alternative to depth interviews or surveys.
- Focus groups may complement other methods in a multi-methods design, but they cannot validate findings from other methods.
- As an ancillary method, focus groups may be used in pre-pilot work to provide a contextual basis for survey design.
- As an ancillary method, focus groups may be used to provide an interpretative aid to (or a critical reappraisal of) survey findings.
- As an ancillary method, focus groups may provide feedback on findings to research participants.
- Focus groups may be a vehicle for extending public participation in the research process.

While focus groups may be used as a main method in studies centrally concerned with norms and meanings (as opposed to the documentation of behaviour, to which they are ill-adapted), focus groups are most frequently encountered as an adjunct to other methods, deliberately chosen to complement, prepare for, or extend other work. In this fashion, focus groups may be used in pre-pilot work to generate preliminary information on new or under-researched norms of behaviour, or to provide contextual data as a resource for subsequent survey design (for example, for the construction of vignettes), or to access the everyday language terms of research subjects. Beyond pilot work, focus groups may be used in an explicit multi-method design; this is frequently termed triangulation, but one should be wary of viewing focus groups as having any validation function: focus groups may serve to elaborate or qualify other findings, but they are not a test, being subject to methodological imperfections like any other method. In contrast to multi-method designs, focus groups may also be a later and separate development, undertaken to clarify a puzzling finding or to contest previous work. Finally, focus groups may be used to democratize the research process by functioning as a forum for public participation; this can occur either through the employment of research participants as group facilitators as well as group members, or through specially convened focus groups to review progress and or findings. So-called indigenous researchers may have advantages for projects over and above the attempted realization of aspirations to democratic practice, but those same cultural features which ease access and understanding for the indigenous researcher may also restrict data collection for a range of reasons from mere over-familiarity through reticence to shame and repugnance. Where research participants are convened in a focus group at the end of a project to consider early findings, this too (like triangulation) has been considered to be a validation exercise ('member validation'), but should more properly be considered (like any multi-method design) to an opportunity to deepen the earlier analysis, rather than a test of it.

EXERCISES

1   In what ways and for what reasons have academic social researchers adopted different focus group practices from the commercial sector?
2   Explain how focus groups may illustrate the ambiguous character of group norms.
3   Why are focus groups better for studying group norms than for studying individual behaviour?
4   Suggest three different ways in which focus groups might usefully be used as an ancillary method alongside a survey investigation of deviant driving.

2

Composition of groups

CONTENTS

As focus group participants are not selected by means of systematic random sampling and the success of the group depends, at least in part, on the dynamics between individuals within the group, there are a range of issues that the researcher has to consider in order to compose and conduct a successful group. Attention must be given to participant characteristics in relation to the topic being discussed and effort and thought must be given to recruitment sources and strategies. Despite these measures, focus groups are unpredictable and the author knows from personal experience careful attention to composition is irrelevant if none of the potential participants turn up to the group! With this in mind this chapter will begin by discussing selection of participants including issues about whether to use groups of strangers or pre-existing groups; this will be followed by a discussion of the number of participants necessary in each group, and factors to be considered when reconvening groups. The chapter will then conclude with a discussion of issues of recruitment and attendance.

Selecting participants

As interaction between participants is a key feature of the focus group method careful consideration of group composition is vital. There has to be sufficient diversity to encourage discussion. However groups that are too heterogeneous may result in conflict and the repression of views of certain individuals. In considering heterogeneity of the group, attention should also be given to the desired depth of information to be achieved from the focus group. Bringing together a very diverse range of people may mean that the range of views, meanings and experiences may be so disparate that no aspect of the topic can be explored in depth. Thus, groups which are too diverse in relation to a particular topic may result in the generation of data that provides an insufficient depth of information.

Conflict may occur in a range of situations where people hold particularly firm and opposing views: you are unlikely to have a successful group if you bring together groups of people with strong allegiance to different political parties, or a group consisting of abortion clinicians and individuals belonging to a pro-life movement. Conducting a focus group with diverse individuals who hold conflicting views can result in high levels of conflict which will crush discussion and inhibit debate and indeed may become quite distressing for individuals involved. Focus group discussion can provoke strong feelings. For example, Kitzinger notes in her research on HIV that any attempts at discussions about risks for gay men were blocked out by strong homophobic clamouring among group members (Kitzinger, 1994b). Such emphatic views on the subject in hand can be can be potentially damaging or threatening for individual members if the composition of the group is badly thought out.

Research goals may require that the researcher conduct groups with a variety of individuals in order to explore a range of views on a given subject. If participants should include those who are likely to hold radically opposed views then it is better to run separate groups, in this way comparison can be made without the need to run disruptive and distressing groups. For example, in a study aiming to explore a range of views towards a proposed change in legislation regarding abortion, groups might consist of: staff in an abortion clinic; women who have experienced an abortion; members of a pro-life movement; women without children; women with young children. These groups might also take into consideration issues such as gender and ethnicity and religiosity in order to inform group composition.

The researcher should also be aware of differentials between participants that may cause some views to be silenced, for example, groups where individuals vary in status and in power. In her research on adolescent smoking in schools Lynn Michell found that some views were being excluded from the focus group discussion (Michell, 1999; Michell and Amos, 1997). Her research indicated that within schools there existed distinct hierarchies of peer groups. When conducting focus groups with pupils from a range of different peer groups she found the views of those in lower status groups were silenced. Michell suggests that in this situation conducting separate individual interviews was of considerable value. If a problem of this kind is identified sufficiently early on in fieldwork then later groups could address this issue, for example by attempting to run groups consisting of individuals from each peer group separately.

Common sense and findings from previous studies within the subject area should be utilized to make informed decisions about the characteristics of participants necessary to have a homogeneous and productive group. Characteristics that are typically considered are sex, ethnicity or race, religion and age as well as background in shared experiences. If resources permit, it is desirable to pilot composition structures. If piloting is not reasonable it should be remembered that focus groups are more flexible than some methods and later groups may be informed by experiences in earlier groups. Researchers should be aware that too much segmentation can lead to potential recruitment problems (Morgan, 1995). If circumstances do not permit a large number of focus groups it may be necessary to narrow the research question and in doing so reduce the number of necessary segments.

Attention to composition is crucial and there are steps that researchers can take to ensure that the likelihood of problems within the group is reduced. However focus groups are a socially dynamic situation and thus to some extent will be unpredictable. Researchers should be aware of the potential problems and prepare strategies for dealing with them (see Chapter 3). As Kitzinger and Barbour (1999) note, there has been an over-emphasis on the degree of control researchers have over the relevant characteristics of individuals in their groups and often the exact composition of the groups will reflect circumstance rather than planning. Despite careful attention and preparation the researcher will not be able to anticipate or necessarily control the direction of the group discussion and thus subjects which appear seemingly innocuous at the outset may stray into difficult areas. Similarly, subjects which appear very 'safe' to the interviewer may in fact be sensitive to participants. As Farquhar and Das argue, all research topics have potential to be sensitive and sensitivity of a topic is not fixed but socially constructed (1999). Groups may contain reticent participants or overbearing dominating members and there may occur instances where particular views and experiences meet with negative responses from other group members. This happened to Duncombe and Marsden in their research on intimate couple relationships. They report:

> However a confirmation that groups may develop powerful and not always benevolent dynamics of their own was provided by several incidents where a group tended to ridicule or pillory its more 'sentimental' or 'romantic'

members, and the ethical problems of our research came dramatically to
the forefront when one participant first became silent and distressed, then
attempted to speak but burst into tears and had to be led away from the
discussion weeping. (Duncombe and Marsden, 1996: 146)

However much careful attention is given to group composition such
eventualities can nevertheless occur. Researchers should be prepared for
these possible occurrences and think through strategies available to them
for managing and dealing with them (see Chapter 3).

Pre-existing or purpose-constructed groups

It has been argued that the notion that focus groups must consist of
strangers is one of the myths associated with focus groups (Morgan and
Krueger, 1993). Groups of strangers have traditionally been favoured by
market research companies as it is felt that where participants know each
other they may be less likely to express taken for granted opinions, views
and experiences than a group of strangers. Group interviews composed
of strangers may also be an economical alternative to individual interviews for commercial researchers. However others have increasingly
recognized the advantages of discussions involving pre-existing social
groups both on practical and epistemological levels.

The decision whether to use pre-existing groups or groups of individuals brought together specifically for the purpose of the focus group
is a debate which has received much attention. Pre-existing groups may
take a variety of forms: a collection of individuals who are no more than
acquaintances (for instance, in certain work settings; see, for example,
Kitzinger, 1994b); family groups (Khan and Manderson, 1992), social
groups (see, for example, Farquhar and Das, 1999), support groups or
friendship groups are all forms of pre-existing groups.

Kitzinger argues, by utilizing friendship groups the researcher may be
able to tap into interaction which approximates to 'naturally occurring'
data (such as may be collected by participant observation). She notes:
'Above all it is useful to work with pre-existing groups because they
provide one of the social contexts within which ideas are formed and
decisions made' (Kitzinger, 1994b: 105).

Research participants who belong to pre-existing social groups may
bring to the interaction comments about shared experiences and events
and may challenge any discrepancies between expressed beliefs and
actual behaviour and generally promote discussion and debate (see, for
example, Kitzinger, 1994b). An example of this is shown in the excerpt
taken from a focus group from Thomas' study of 'holiday romance'. The
group consisted of a group of female friends who had travelled abroad
on holiday together.

Int.: Do you think that's usual for holiday romances [that they last beyond the holiday]?

Jodie: Now and again, the law of averages say twenty five out of a hundred meet and say seventy five don't. You met this bloke didn't you?

Tanya: Oh yeah yeah, God yeah !!!! Course I did, yeah in Greece. And we stayed, well we're still in contact now and how long ago was that, two year, a year ago.

Jodie: Yeah a year ago.

Tanya: And we used to see each other, well, every other month for say . . . well we're supposed to phone each other now as friends but that's it cos he's got a girlfriend and I've got a boyfriend, so you know we still keep in touch, we send birthday cards and things.

Jodie: Buy each other really expensive presents but they see each other as friends!! [laugh] just friends!

This extract illustrates the way discussion is generated as one friend reminds another about an experience relevant to the discussion that might otherwise have been overlooked. She goes on to challenge behaviour that she sees inconsistent with the construction of the relationship as one between 'friends'. This discussion is enabled by individual participants' prior knowledge of each other and as such could not occur in a group consisting of strangers.

Pre-existing groups may be advantageous where participation in the group involves disclosure of a potentially stigmatizing condition or status such as being HIV positive or homosexual, particularly if this condition or behaviour is normally invisible or covert (Farquhar and Das, 1999). Farquhar and Das argue that in such situations the researcher has to be aware that, unlike other research methods, focus groups involve individuals identifying themselves not just to a researcher but to other members of the group. By recruiting from pre-existing social groups where the characteristic or status is the basis of the group membership (for example, a group for HIV positive women) then issues of disclosure of a potentially stigmatizing status can be overcome. Furthermore, recruitment via a pre-existing formal group also reduces the need for individuals to disclose names or contact addresses and phone numbers, thus further protecting participant anonymity (Farquhar and Das, 1999).

Pre-existing groups can also have major practical benefits, which can be of no small significance to the researcher. Recruiting a group that is part of an established social network can reduce recruitment effort for the researcher as she or he can potentially contact group members through one individual group member, rather than contacting each group member separately (see section on recruitment, this chapter). Furthermore, it is possible that pre-existing groups may result in reduced attrition rates. This may be due to the fact that attendance at a group may be less likely to seem daunting to individual participants if the group consists of people of whom they have prior knowledge. There may also be a sense of shared obligation to attend (in contrast to a group of strangers who may feel less responsible about turning up in the – all too often mistaken – belief that it does not matter if they do not turn up to the group as other group members will). Thomas' experience of recruiting for focus groups for the study of holiday romance showed that those groups consisting of friends were both less time consuming and labour intensive to recruit and also more likely to result in groups where the majority of recruited individuals attended.

Whilst pre-existing groups have advantages, this is not to say that focus groups consisting of strangers cannot also be successful. Focus groups consisting of strangers may potentially have the additional advantage of allowing people to speak more freely and openly than they would in a pre-existing social group (the sense of confessing all to the stranger on the train) without fear of repercussions after the group is over (see section on over-disclosure below). Furthermore, processes of individual group members challenging each other and pointing out contradictions in expressed views and behaviour can still occur in groups where individuals have no prior knowledge of each other (Wilkinson, 1998). Indeed it is argued that such challenges and questioning may be more direct and probing than a 'sensitive' researcher may feel comfortable asking (Wilkinson, 1998). The quote below from a group discussion between four teenage girls clearly illustrates how group dynamics work to encourage members to explain and justify statements and seemingly contradictory views that are expressed in the focus group setting:

> *Treena*: But if a bloke asks you for sex, what do you do?
> *Brid*: I'd tell him to go off and have a wank!
> *Stella*: You dirty thing!
> *Kate*: It's wrong, you ought to get married in a white dress.
> *Stella*: But I don't think it is – if you like the bloke why not? Why wait until you are married?
> *Treena*: She's talking – I bet she's done it!
> *Kate*: You ought to sleep with a bloke if you love him and he asked you to.
> *Stella*: But you just said that you had to get married in white!
> (Griffin, 1986: 182–183 quoted in Wilkinson, 1998)

However, groups of strangers may be less cohesive than those consisting of individuals with pre-existing social links. It may take more time for the group to 'warm up' and here the creation of effective focusing exercises may be particularly important (see Chapter 3). Experience also suggests that bringing together groups of strangers can be problematic in some instances as they appear to be less likely to attend the group (see later section on recruitment, this chapter).

Problems of over-disclosure

A further issue that impacts on the selection of participants is that of over-disclosure. Over-disclosure refers to a situation where respondents impart more information, express views or declare experiences in the group setting that they subsequently may feel uncomfortable about revealing (Morgan and Krueger, 1993). The very nature of focus groups may mean that there may be a particular propensity for participants to reveal information about which they would otherwise remain silent. Over-disclosure can happen when individuals get carried away in the heat of a discussion or debate. Morgan and Krueger (1993) warn that sometimes the thrill of talking about a taboo topic may lead participants to disclose personal information that is beyond the legitimate aim of the research. Over-disclosure can impact on selection of participants as it is a problem that can potentially be exacerbated in pre-existing groups. In pre-existing groups regretted or reluctant revelations can be precipitated by other group members, for example where participants make reference to a personal view or experience of another group member that that individual does not feel comfortable divulging within that particular group setting. Similarly, in pre-existing groups, spur of the moment disclosures about issues or events unknown to some, or all other group members are not confined to the focus group discussion, but can be referred to and impact upon everyday relationships after the group is over. For example, a focus group concerned with sexual relationships might result in a member, believed by other members to be in a long-term monogamous relationship, to discuss her experience of recently contracting a sexually transmitted disease through a casual sexual encounter. This disclosure might impact on the group members' perceptions and feelings towards this participant. In addition, as the researcher cannot control confidentiality outside the group setting, there is the risk that this information might spread through a pre-existing group and reach other members of this social group including her long-term partner. Indeed some group members who might have a friendship with the participant and her partner may feel they face a dilemma as to whether they ought to tell him of her infidelity. Thus the content of the focus group discussion can have consequences beyond the temporal and social confines of the focus group itself.

Such openness and revelation can have positive consequences. For example, individuals may gain reassurance when realizing that feelings, behaviours and uncertainties are shared by others in their group (Duncombe and Marsden, 1996; Farquhar and Das, 1999; Madriz, 1998; Stewart and Shamdasani, 1990). Such a process of reassurance and exchange of information was found by Farquhar in her research concerned with lesbian sexual health. She reported that after many of the focus groups' participants commented on the value of the sessions and their enjoyment in taking part and how supportive they found the discussion (Farquhar and Das, 1999).

Despite these potential positive consequences, the problem of over-disclosure highlights the fact that assurances of confidentiality on the part of the researcher are limited in focus group research, in that information is shared among members of the group over whom the researcher has little control. Strategies can be adopted to reduce the likelihood of potential problems such as emphasizing the voluntary nature of the research and giving respondents the opportunity to view and amend transcripts of the discussion before the data is analysed and written up. To an extent, problems of over-disclosure can be alleviated by ensuring that each participant is aware of the topic of study before they agree to participate in the group. Ensuring such awareness is, of course, only adhering to the good ethical practice of seeking 'informed consent'. However the very unpredictability and dynamic nature of focus groups (which is also part of their attraction) means that the researcher can never be entirely sure which direction the discussion is going to take. Researchers should be sensitive to situations where individuals may become distressed or uncomfortable and intervene where necessary (see Chapter 3). For some research topics and some participants, it may be considered more appropriate to use groups of strangers, where individuals can speak freely without fear of any repercussions of intimate disclosures once the group is over. In order to assess the necessity of using groups consisting of strangers, attention should be given to both the topic and the characteristics of the individuals to participate in groups. Some pre-existing social groups, may not, for example, be very supportive of individual difference or eccentricity outside the of the group setting. Other groups may find particular topics of high sensitivity. In such instances the researcher may decide that focus groups consisting of strangers will minimize post-group discomfort and problems.

Why size does matter

Focus group texts have typically advised groups consisting of between six and eight participants as the optimum size for focus group discussion. However groups have been reported that have ranged in size from as small as three participants to fourteen (see Pugsley, 1996; Thomas, 1999). As with any research method, decisions will be made within the context of inevitable practical constraints. The size of the group may be decided by logistic issues, for example, exploring staff satisfaction in small businesses where there are only a small number of employees will necessarily define the limits of the size of your group. In some instances researchers will simply be limited by the number of people that turn up (see, for example, Madriz, 1998; Thomas, 1999). Despite these factors it is important to make informed decisions and targets to aim for regarding the number of participants felt to be optimum and endeavour, where possible, to meet these numbers.

The optimum size of the group may reflect the characteristics of participants as well as the topic being discussed. Groups of a small size have been successfully used in studies of sensitive behaviour (see, for example, Basch, 1987; Duncombe and Marsden, 1996; Maxwell and Boyle, 1995; Nix et al., 1988, Thomas, 1999), older and disabled people (Quine and Cameron, 1995) and are favoured by some researchers (see Barbour and Kitzinger, 1999). Morgan (1995) argues that small groups may be desirable with certain types of research topics or certain types of participants. Small groups may be advantageous if the topic is a very complex one or if you are dealing with experts or people in authority who might respond negatively if they feel that they have not had enough time to express their view (Morgan, 1995). Focus groups of a small size were successfully used by Thomas in a study of holiday romance, with the smallest group consisting of three individuals. While this a smaller number than is typically advocated by methods texts, it appeared that for this specific topic with this particular group small numbers may have facilitated greater discussion. Ethnographies of young women's friend-ship have shown that girls friendship groups are typically clustered around best friends and small groups (Hey, 1997; McRobbie and Garber, 1976). It could therefore be argued that if small groups are more typical patterns of interaction for women then these may be productive for focus group purposes. Indeed the researcher may be confronted by difficulties in recruiting large friendship groups of young women. Quine and Cameron (1995) in their research with disabled elderly people also advocate the use of small numbers for this group. They argue that sufficient space is needed to accommodate mobility aids and participants must be able to be seated close enough to each other to see and hear each other adequately. For these reasons, they argue numbers should be kept low, advising five to six participants as desirable with this group.

While groups of a smaller size are advocated by a number of researchers, it should be noted that groups consisting of a small number of individuals can potentially result in limited discussion and are at risk of cancellation if just one or two participants fail to turn up. It is quite usual for groups to include shy or reticent participants, these will have more impact on the potential discussion in a group of a smaller size and may mean that the discussion that arises is more like a question and answer situation with an interviewer rather than a discussion among group members which gains its own momentum (Green and Hart, 1999).

Larger groups can also present problems. In general, groups which are too large can become difficult to moderate and may be frustrating for participants if they feel that they have not had adequate time to express their views and opinions. For example, a group that consists of nine participants plus one facilitator which lasts for one-and-a-half hours, does not allow each individual much opportunity or time to air their views and opinions on the particular subject matter. A discussion in which participants want to join in enthusiastically can turn into chaos in groups that are large in number (Green and Hart, 1999). In large groups there is also the risk that the more outgoing and vociferous members of the group will dominant the interaction so that only a small proportion of those present are actually contributing to the discussion.

Finally, in considering the size of the group, it should also be noted that the number of participants in the group will have significant implications for the transcription of recordings of the group discussion for subsequent analysis. The importance of assigning identifiers to text within the transcript is discussed in detail in Chapter 4. However, in general, the more participants in the group the more difficult it becomes for the transcriber to attribute sets of interaction to specific individuals (this is particularly true if the person transcribing the tape was not present at the discussion or if the tape is transcribed by the researcher a considerable time after the group has taken place). For academic research, successful analysis will, in part, be dependent on the ability to accurately attribute specific sets of interaction to individual group members and this may have implications for decisions regarding the optimum size for the group.

Whatever the size group selected, it is standard practice to 'over-recruit' in anticipation that all participants do not turn up. However care should be taken to ensure that this strategy does not result in a group of an unmanageably large size (see the section on recruitment, later in this chapter).

How many groups?

The number of participants or number of focus groups and the value and significance of the findings of the groups cannot and should not be deduced by a statistical calculation as is necessary in more quantitative methods. Rather the number of focus groups will inevitably reflect the research plan including which sub-groups you might want to target, which groups views you might want to compare, the variability of responses, as well as the inevitable influences of time and money. In general the more segmented your groups are (for example by age, gender and sexuality) the more groups will be necessary (Morgan, 1995). Focus groups are labour intensive in recruitment, transcription and analysis, therefore, where possible, numbers should be kept down to the bare minimum.

Reconvening groups

In certain study designs it may be seen as advantageous to reconvene a group for a second meeting. This may be desirable to follow up ambiguities discovered after initial analysis or confirm preliminary findings (Bloor, 1997). Preliminary groups may also be used to explore the suitability of questions and language as meaningful to participants or the effectiveness of focusing exercises for provoking relevant debate. While there are advantages of a research design that advocates the use of groups in different stages there are many practical issues relating to this that make it problematic. These difficulties are largely similar to the problems confronted when convening the group initially (see the section on recruitment, this chapter). Furthermore, in many instances it may be impossible to bring an identical group together for a second discussion. Social groupings are dynamic and circumstances of individuals may change over time. For example, a study considering how the views of schoolchildren on sex education may change as they go through school may face difficulties when reconvening groups: some children may change school and no longer be available for participation; others may be absent through sickness or truanting. The children involved in the initial group may also have changed classes so that convening the group in a suitable period for children in a variety of classes may also prove difficult.

Rather than attempting to reconvene groups, it is usually more feasible to include in the study design different groups which can inform analysis at a variety of levels. In this way methods and analysis can be qualified and developed without the difficulties associated with reconvening groups. An example of this strategy can be found in the work of Middleton et al. (1994). Their study aimed to assess family expenditure on children and to define and assess the cost of children in Britain in the 1990s and by doing so, assess the rate of childhood poverty. Focus groups were conducted with parents 'who had the major responsibility for day-to-day expenditures on children' (who in the event, all turned out to be mothers). This study design included the use of groups in three stages. An initial set of 'orientation' groups were held with the aim of ensuring that 'the ideas and concepts used in the later stages of the project would be informed and understood by the parents' (Middleton et al., 1994: 153). These groups were asked to compile lists of items their children had or consumed under particular expenditure categories (for example, food, clothes, activities). These groups then discussed the difficulties of putting together these lists along with other relevant issues such as pressure on parents and budgeting strategies; thus aiding development of instrumentation for the next set of groups. The second phase of the groups aimed to produce an agreed list of minimum essential requirements for children of a range of ages. Prior to the group these mothers completed a set of instrumentation on the particular budget area that was to be covered by that group and these were used to inform discussion. The final third set of groups was to check on the list of minimum essential requirements for children of different ages produced by the second stage of groups. This design allowed a process of qualification and deepening of findings of earlier groups through the feedback information to parents, without the difficulties of attempting to reconvene identical groups.

Recruitment

Once group composition has been decided then the required participants must be recruited. This can be done in a number of ways. Systematic random sampling is less important here because the aim of a focus group is not to make generalizations to a population in the same way that large-scale quantitative methods may have as their goal. Findings of focus groups do need to be generalizable and this might be addressed simply by the coverage of the range of the population. However this generalizability also needs to be offset against other aims. Purposive or theoretical sampling can be used where researchers can be guided by their particular research questions and key characteristics that are considered relevant and individuals recruited accordingly.

Where focus groups are aimed at developing questionnaires or understanding responses to questions participants should reflect the respondents to the survey. Where focus groups are used in conjunction with a survey, respondents can be drawn from the survey sample to participate in focus groups. In a study design of this type focus group participants can be randomly selected from the survey sample based on any combination of specific data that has been collected in the survey (for example, age, socio-economic group, health status, etc.). Pre-existing surveys may also be used to randomly select eligible individuals to participate in focus groups which may be unrelated to the survey. With this method of recruitment it is important that consent is given by survey respondents to be recontacted for the purpose of being involved in further research.

Recruitment strategies will need to incorporate screening for eligibility. A pre-existing sampling frame may be used so that initial contact is only made with those individuals who are eligible for participation in the group. For example, Thomas (1999) used class registration lists to randomly select pupils to take part in focus groups exploring the impact of a smoking intervention in schools. Registration lists were taken only from those classes in those schools which were participating in the intervention thus ineligible pupils were automatically screened out in this selection process. This method may also be employed if focus groups are used in conjunction with a survey (see Chapter 1) where a representative sample of individuals can be drawn from the survey sample. Data collected for the purposes of the survey (such as age, sex, social class) can be utilized to select appropriate individuals for contact for focus group participation.

If a pre-existing sampling frame or pool of respondents is not available then participants can be recruited by approaching them individually at a chosen sampling site. This strategy is often adopted by market research companies where researchers stand in strategic locations such as busy shopping centres and approach individuals to take part in research. Appropriate sampling sites for this method will be dependent on access and the characteristics required of group participants, for example, for a study of the elderly a researcher could attempt to recruit outside a post office on pension day. For Thomas' (1999) study of holiday romance a regional airport was utilized as a site for recruitment as participants of focus groups were required to have recently travelled abroad without a partner.

If eligibility criterion for participation in the group is not particularly specific or detailed (for example, you simply wish to recruit mothers of children under two years of age) then screening can take place verbally. However, it is usually the case that sensitivity to characteristics important for a homogeneous group will mean that eligibility criterion might be based on a number of factors (age of child, marital status and social class). In these situations it may be advisable for individuals to complete a short questionnaire or screening form which will allow the researcher to assess their eligibility. This method may be particularly appropriate if eligibility or group allocation is dependent on issues that are of potential sensitivity, such as household income. In these cases individuals may be more comfortable communicating these details (and indeed researchers more comfortable asking these questions) by means of a short self-complete questionnaire rather than verbally, face-to-face.

This method of approaching potential participants individually can be very labour intensive and time consuming and can be contracted out to professional recruiters (see for example, Middleton et al., 1994). However financial resources do not always extend to this and often researchers are left to their own efforts. It also may not always be possible to negotiate access to your preferred sampling site. However this approach may be necessary if there is no existing sampling frame for the group in question. If this method proves ineffective other methods of recruitment can be adopted such as those which rely on self-selection, for example through flyers or local advertisements in appropriate locations or publications. This latter method can be an effective way of recruiting low prevalence or stigmatized groups.

Recruitment via an intermediary

A further strategy that can be particularly successful for the recruitment of groups is to contact individual group members through an inter-mediary. Recruitment via an intermediary can occur in 'snowball sampling', for example, where an eligible individual is approached by the researcher at a chosen recruitment site and the individual is then willing to recruit eligible members of their own existing network to take part in the research. This method can also be used where one member or leader of a more formal pre-existing group (such as a group for arthritis suffers or a pre-natal group) is approached to recruit a number of other group members to take part in the research. Researchers may utilize their own existing social networks to recruit for focus groups in this manner. The person who acts as a contact point may attend the focus group or may simply act as an intermediary who is associated with the group but who will not necessarily take part in the discussion.

Recruitment via this method has the obvious advantage of reduction of recruitment effort: the need to communicate primarily through one person rather than four or more greatly decreases the labour necessary on the part of the researcher. However this benefit must be juxtaposed with the potential loss of control this arrangement gives the researcher and the fact that the existence of the group will be heavily dependent on the goodwill and efforts of the contact person. The loss of goodwill or enthusiasm of that person might jeopardize the existence of the entire group. Furthermore the intermediary may act as an unwanted 'screening device' selecting out certain members of the group from participation. For example, if conducting research on smoking among school pupils it would be unwise to ask a head teacher or form teacher to select pupils to take part in the group: desire to present a favourable public image of the school may result in a group of non-smoking prefects, with smokers and those pupils considered more 'deviant' being excluded from the research.

If recruiting via a group member or leader it is important that the researcher takes steps to ensure that research guidelines are adhered to. Such guidelines include insuring that each potential participant receives adequate information about the study and each individual gives informed consent to participation. Informed consent is of course a crucial issue in research ethics. By contacting a group through an inter-mediary this process might be inadvertently bypassed (see Farquhar and Das, 1999). Individual participants may not receive full details of the research study or may in some way feel cajoled or pressured to parti-cipate as a member of this pre-existing group. Not only is this unethical it also has potential implications for their participation in the discussion. Those members who are present at the focus group through some sense of obligation (either to the group or research organization) may make reluctant and reticent participants and this may impact on the quality of the data generated. An example of the problems of recruiting via an intermediary is given by Kitzinger and Barbour (1999) where a group consisting of members of a football club was set up by a market research company for the purpose of discussing sexual abuse. However when Kitzinger arrived to facilitate the group she found that the men had been told by the group contact that they were going to discuss football hooliganism, the group contact having found it difficult to recruit mem-bers in any other way. This arrangement may also prove detrimental if the intermediary is in a powerful position relative to the participants. Their involvement may render it problematic to distance the researcher's interests from that of the organization and this may limit open and honest debate and discussion within the group.

The researcher should give clear guidelines to their contact person including the minimum and maximum number required to be recruited for participation in group. The implementation of eligibility criteria should also be considered. If your contact person is the co-ordinator of a mixed sex group of arthritis sufferers and you are only interested in women's experiences of arthritis then you must be clear from the onset about your requirements for participation in the group.

Where formal pre-existing groups are involved in focus group discussions the researcher may utilize the fact that the group have a regular meeting time and place and arrange to make use of this for the purposes of the focus group discussion. For example, a researcher attempting to explore individuals' experiences of attempting to lose weight might contact a slimming group and arrange the focus group immediately prior to or after the usual weekly meeting in the same venue. This is obviously advantageous in that it is likely to reduce attrition. However, this situation also reduces the amount of control the researcher has over the research. It is advisable for the researcher to visit the discussion group venue prior to the group taking place in order to assess its suitability. This should include a consideration of factors such as size of the room, noise levels in the room, likelihood of interruption and so on.

Ensuring attendance

Recruitment for focus groups can present particular difficulties for researchers. Indeed some would argue that it is the most common source of failure in focus group research (Morgan, 1995). The focus group researcher faces the burden of not only identifying willing and eligible respondents, but also ensuring that they attend the group. This is no easy task, and despite over-recruiting it is not unheard of that not a single participant will turn up (see, for example, Madriz, 1998; Thomas, 1999). While there is a limit to the degree of control the researcher has over the respondent, every effort should be made to reduce the likelihood that individuals fail to turn up to the group meeting. Records should be kept of details of participants, including any special transport requirements necessary to participate in the group. Meeting potential participants can increase their chances of attending the group as the researcher will not be seen as a complete stranger. Meetings prior to the group also give respondents an immediate opportunity to ask any questions they might have. Participants should be given appointment cards and the researcher should be prepared to make reminder phone calls and send reminder letters if the date of the focus group is a significant distance from the date of recruitment. Information sheets and a contact number for the researcher should also be provided so that respondents are able to contact the researcher with any queries or give notice in advance if their circumstances change and they become unable to attend the group.

The use of payment for participation in qualitative research is rarely considered, usually through fear that this will introduce bias. However it has been argued that the dangers of making payments can be outweighed by gains in reducing bias and compensating for power differentials between researcher and researched (Thompson, 1998). Indeed it is quite usual to offer participants a small amount of money to cover any 'out-of-pocket' expenses (such as train fare) incurred as a result of attending the group (see Chapter 3). It is also possible to offer other, nonmonetary, incentives such as running the focus group in a pleasing location and offering participants a selection of food and drinks. The psychological incentives for participating in the group may also be stressed such as the opportunity for facilitating interaction among peers (Morgan, 1995).

Certain groups may be harder to recruit than others. It has already been noted where groups consist of individuals who have a social relationship outside the context of the research then there is likely to be a lower attrition rate. Attrition rates may also be reduced with more 'formal' pre-existing groups where existing meeting times and venues are utilized for the purposes of the focus group discussion.

While recruitment and ensuring attendance can be problematic for the focus group researcher these problems can be overcome through creative thinking and (sometimes considerable) effort. An example of a study where the researcher faced particular recruitment challenges is Madriz's (1998) research with 'lower socio-economic status' Latina women exploring fear of crime. Madriz reports that gaining participation of this group was a challenge because: 'Some feel apprehensive, especially if they are recent immigrants or undocumented women, live on welfare, or engage in any nonnormative behaviour such as alternative family living arrangements or working in the informal economy' (1998: 120).

Madriz experienced problems with 'no show' at her groups when out of 15 women who agreed to participant only a few turned up. Madriz attributes these problems in part to aspects of the Latino culture, where women have sole responsibility for child care and domestic work and are expected to be available to their partners and children, giving them less control over their time than some other groups. The cultural stress on good relationships also may have encouraged women to say 'yes' to the invitation to attend. In order to overcome these problems and ease recruitment and maximize attendance Madriz utilized personal social networks such as students and individuals involved in community organizations and maximized personal contact with recruiters, answering questions and providing information about the study. Difficulties of attendance were overcome by use of incentives, for example, some participants were given a small sum of money for participation in the group or where this was considered culturally unacceptable other incentives were provided, for example, giving a presentation about violence against women. Madriz also arranged transport to groups, made several last minute 'reminder calls' to participants, offered to conduct groups in Spanish and conducted groups in settings familiar to the women (see Chapter 3). Thus she managed to successfully conduct focus groups with Latina women of a range of ages and socio-economic status.

While ensuring members turn up is a particular issue for the researcher planning focus groups, it should not be forgotten that focus groups can encourage participation from individuals or groups who may be reluctant to be involved in a one-to-one interview. Groups may be reassuring in the sense that there is safety in numbers and this may be particularly true of groups where individuals share a particular status or experience or where the group consists of individuals who already have social knowledge of each other.

Conclusion

Decisions regarding the selection and targeting of participants will necessarily reflect the nature of the topic to be studied and the specific purpose of the group and will reflect epistemological concerns about the nature of the data being collected as well as more practical issues regarding ease of recruitment and access. When considering group composition, care should be taken to avoid groups that consist of individuals too diverse to obtain a sufficient depth of information on the research topic. Groups should also be avoided that consist of individuals with such conflicting views that the resultant discussion might cause distress to individual members.

Focus groups may consist of pre-existing social groups, both formal (for example, a support group for those suffering with depression) and informal (for example, a group of friends). Pre-existing groups have the advantage of providing a more 'natural' setting for discussion and tend to ease recruitment efforts. Groups of strangers can also be used for focus groups and may be advantageous where the researcher is concerned with 'over-disclosure' which in pre-existing groups might have reper-cussions once the research is over.

Size of group may be dictated by logistic issues and will in part reflect the nature of the topic and the characteristics of the individuals involved in the group. Smaller groups are favoured by some researchers as they may be a more 'normal' setting for discussion and allow sufficient time for considerable input from each group member. Larger groups may prove to be frustrating for individual group members if they feel they have not had sufficient time to express their views on the given subject, may be harder to facilitate and may result in problems during transcrip-tion and subsequent analysis.

Recruitment strategy for focus group participants can take a variety of forms. Focus group members may be selected from pre-existing survey samples, or other sampling frames (such as a school register). Where such a participant 'pool' does not exist it may be necessary for the researcher to recruit at an appropriate recruitment site or utilize strategically placed flyers or advertisements to recruit participants. Recruitment effort may be dramatically reduced if the researcher is able to recruit via an intermediary who is part of a formal or informal pre-existing group whose members you wish to take part in the research. However, this method leaves the researcher dependent on the goodwill of the intermediary and reduces control over the process of recruitment. If recruiting via an intermediary, care should be taken to ensure informed consent is obtained from all participants.

Ensuring individuals attend the focus group is a particular problem for the focus group researcher and it is standard practice to recruit more participants than you actually need in the assumption that a number will not turn up on the day. Attendance is likely to be higher if the group consists of a pre-existing social group. Utilizing an established meeting venue and time for a formal pre-existing group can also improve attendance. Other strategies include offers of transport to group and use of reminder phone calls and letters. While the researcher may face difficulties ensuring attendance this should not result in the possibility of focus groups being ruled out. Indeed individuals may be more likely to attend a group than a one-to-one interview as they may feel reassurance that they are with a group of individuals who share a particular characteristic or experience and that attention is on the group rather than the individual.

EXERCISES

1   Imagine you have been commissioned by your Health Education Authority to conduct some research into people's eating habits and their ideas about what constitutes a healthy meal. Devise a research design to include:
    a) details of group composition
    b) number of groups
    c) views on optimum number of participants.

2   You are planning a study to explore the views of single women over 35 years old on 'sexual reputation'. How would recruit this group? What strategies would you use to ensure attendance?

3

Preparation and conduct

CONTENTS

Most of the issues addressed in this chapter concerning the preparation and conduct of focus groups take on a rather different character when virtual focus groups are considered. Venue and audio recording are irrelevancies, but issues of length and facilitation are crucial. To avoid confusion therefore, issues in the preparation and conduct of virtual focus groups are discussed separately within Chapter 5. What follows here applies only to 'live' or 'real life' focus groups.

Choice of venue

As we saw in the previous chapter, successful recruitment may depend on the accessibility of the venue to participants. For this reason it is important for focus groups with a work group membership to be held at the worksite (if they can be held in work time without loss of earnings, so much the better for recruitment!). Bloor's feedback focus groups with staff in his therapeutic community study were held in the same room in each community as the staff meetings and probably benefited from the association in that members treated the groups in a serious and business-like manner. It was true that in each community the senior staff member tended to assume a chairing role, as they would in a staff meeting, but this is perhaps only disadvantageous if the chair fails to understand the purpose of the meeting and interferes with the researcher's facilitator role.

What applies to workgroups also applies to student groups. Frankland's adolescent groups on smoking (Frankland and Bloor, 1999) were run in school time. Schools may be quite pleased to have an outsider take over a timetable slot for a number of sessions, if the topic of the research can be related to a curriculum topic, as in Frankland's study, where smoking and health was a recurrent topic in PSE (or 'civics') lessons. But by the same token, schools will be reluctant to find time within their crowded curricula for research that is not curriculum-related and will prefer to avoid any possible distractions in examination periods. Recruiting schoolchildren to take part in research *outside* school time can be very difficult and parents may be more likely to withhold their content: many children have substantial out-of-school commitments (clubs, sports, training, music practice, visits to other family and relatives, etc.) and transport must be organized. However, there are also some disadvantages to holding focus groups in schools. One such problem is that school lesson periods are typically shorter by half than the running time of a normal focus group: unless a double-lesson timetable slot can be found, then the group faces the unpopular option of running into break-times or lunchtimes. There is also the obvious difficulty that (no matter how assiduously the researcher has sought the informed consent of participants) the classroom setting, the PSE timetable slot, and so on, may lead pupils to treat the focus group as just another lesson to be endured: no collectivity on earth is more practiced at mute resistance than a group of schoolchildren.

The chosen institutional venue should be free from interruptions or surveillance with no non-participating staff member wandering in to make phone calls or coffee, no teacher in the classroom. Too much background noise will spoil the audio recording. Sometimes, there may be no suitable public room available. Bloor recently conducted focus groups with officers and crew on a merchant vessel at sea where accommodation space was at a premium so the groups had to be conducted in one of the larger cabins.

Aside from groups in workplaces and schools, some other kinds of groups may be readily accommodated. A pensioners' lunch club, for example, may form a group directly after lunch has been cleared away. A 'mothers-and-toddlers' group may form themselves into a focus group as part of their normal activities in the hall in which they are based. But greater difficulties are associated with the choice of venue of certain other groups. The possibility of holding an ex-patients' feedback focus group in a pub was discussed in Bloor's therapeutic community study (publicans will often set aside the use of a private room at no charge in the expectation of extra trade), but it was discounted because some of the possible attenders had been referred to the therapeutic community with a drink problem. In the end, one ex-patient offered the use of his bedsit. Just as ex-problem drinkers should not meet in a pub, so also elderly and/or disabled participants should not have to negotiate stairs and may need to have transport arranged to and from the venue.

Bloor's ex-patients from the therapeutic community study had come to know him well over months of fieldwork and had kept in touch with him socially in several cases after they had been discharged as patients. Indeed, their reasons for participating in the focus group were partly to do with their personal relationships with the researcher; the only difficulty with the choice of venue was literally that of finding a suitable room. But Thomas' (1999) group members had simply met her briefly in an airport baggage reclaim area, there was no pre-existing personal relationship. In this case, the arrangement to use a seminar room in the university was much more appropriate and reinforced the neutral scientific status of the enquiry into a topic (sexual relationships while holidaying abroad) which might otherwise be considered of prurient interest; the university was also centrally located and readily found by those travelling in from outside the city. The bare and unwelcoming character of the average university seminar room can be modified (slightly) by the offer of coffee and biscuits. Community Centres comprise another popular venue, although many of their meeting rooms are regularly booked by local clubs and organizations.

Whatever the venue chosen, it needs to be recognized that the venue itself will impact on the data collected. If the group is held in the home of one of the participants, then that participant is likely to display host/hostess-like traits in their contributions to the discussion. Green and Hart (1999) showed that the formality of the group discussions they held with children, varied systematically with the formality of the setting (primary schools versus children's Saturday Club versus Cub Scout group): in the primary schools children would police each other, hold up their hands for permission to speak, and so on, whereas in the Saturday Club they would laugh, joke, interrupt and even fight each other and would casually drift off in mid-discussion to play elsewhere. There is no such thing as a neutral venue for a focus group.

Pre-group self-completion questionnaires

Some basic socio-demographic information such as age and marital status may be required for analysis purposes and this may be most appropriately collected immediately before the group starts. It is also a convenient time-filler in the awkward minutes before a group starts and where one is waiting for possible late arrivals. It may be convenient to attach a short information sheet and (if required by a research ethics committee) an informed consent form along with the self-complete questionnaires. The collection of self-completion data from group members may be particularly important where focus groups are part of a multi-method research design. In such cases it is likely that the researcher will want to establish how far and in what ways the group members differ from other samples generated by the other methods used in the design. This may involve the collection of more than just socio-demographic background data. For example, in a health study it may be relevant to establish not just the age profile of group members relative to those participating in a contemporaneous survey, but it may be relevant (depending on the precise study topic) to repeat in the pre-group self-completion questionnaire some of the information sought in the survey on (say) smoking patterns and drink consumption, or to ask group members to complete a short health status screening instrument such as the SF-36 or the Nottingham Health Profile. The collection of such self-completion data from focus group members is only superfluous where the focus group members form a sub-sample of a larger survey sample. In such cases, sample respondents may be asked as part of the survey if they are willing to be recontacted in pursuit of further information. The data supplied by individuals in the survey can then be linked to the focus group data on an unnamed basis by use of the individual's survey number. If one is sub-sampling from a pre-existing sample, it is an easy matter to address possible questions of focus group sample bias by representative sampling, or stratified sampling, or quota sampling, as desired.

However, a pre-group self-completion questionnaire may serve a quite different function from those of the compilation of socio-demographic background data and the documentation of possible sample bias. It is also possible to use the pre-group questionnaire to check for the possibility of initial differences of viewpoint on the study topic within the focus group. Sometimes these initial differences will be expressed in the focus group and one or other contrary position may be modified in the course of the discussion. On other occasions, a member of the group may hold a different viewpoint but their dissent may be entirely silent. In a focus group on HIV/AIDS held among a group of local residents one of the group may have a different viewpoint from the others based on the fact that they have a relative who is HIV-positive, but they may not wish to reveal this to their fellow workers because they fear possible stigma by association. While it is good research practice to check for such self-censorship, it should not be assumed to be an extensive phenomenon. In such a group of residents from the same Glasgow estate, facilitated by Kitzinger (1994a), two women, who were much less concerned than other group members about casual HIV transmission, were perfectly prepared to report to the group, in one case, that a brother was a drug injector and, in another case, that a relative was gay.

It is obviously to the advantage of the researcher to have some knowledge of these underlying issues in interpreting the unfolding events of the focus group, to know when there has been silent dissent, or when the developing discussion has caused a modification of initial viewpoints. The researcher's purpose in documenting these under-currents is obviously quite different from that of collecting basic socio-demographic background data, but the two purposes can be usefully combined in one pre-group questionnaire. It is for this reason that we suggest that questionnaires are administered pre-group rather than post-group. It is possible to administer both pre- and post-group question-naires, but some group members may find this a bit excessive. And although a post-group questionnaire can be usefully combined with the end debriefing (see below), it is clearly advantageous to document any initial disagreements of viewpoint *before* the group starts, rather than afterwards. So, if one dual-purpose questionnaire is to be completed, it is better that it be completed at the beginning. And if two questionnaires are deemed absolutely necessary, it is better that the post-group ques-tionnaire be taken away for subsequent completion by members at a later date and posting back in a pre-paid envelope.

Audio recording

Some of the early reports of focus group methods suggested that a professional facilitator be employed to run the focus groups and the academic researcher concentrate on manual recording of the group interaction. While it is of course true that the quality of the data collected owes much to the skills of the facilitator, professional facilitators are now rarely employed in academic focus group research (as opposed to commercial market research). Where the group is facilitated by some-one other than the academic researcher, it is generally led by an 'indi-genous' researcher (see Chapters 1and 6) collaborating with the academic researcher, either in a conscious spirit of co-participation, or because the group is to be conducted in a language in which the academic researcher is not fluent. Just as the professional facilitator has been superseded, so also the need for manual recording has disappeared as audio-recording equipment has progressively improved in quality since the reel-to-reel recorders used in the 1970s. Nevertheless, it is important to ensure that precautions are taken to ensure that the recording is of sufficient quality to allow a transcript to be made.

Audio-recording equipment that is suitable for recording one-to-one interviews may not always produce a recording of sufficient quality when used in group settings. The microphone component is obviously crucial. Audio recorders with mikes containing an automatic volume control (a popular feature of models marketed for domestic use) should be avoided: they will adjust their volume to cope with a loud speaker and, if the next speaker is quieter, their initial utterances will be lost before the volume is automatically adjusted upward. If the researcher is unhappy with the quality of the built-in mike, then an external, multi-directional mike attachment should be used, but care should be taken to ensure that both the mike attachment and the cassette recorder are switched on (the mike attachment being often operated by a separate solar battery).

The cassette recorder should be so placed as to ensure that all members of the group are being adequately recorded. It may be advantageous to experiment with the recorder at the start of the group by asking each member in turn to identify themselves by their first name and then playing the recording back to check on audibility. This initial experiment may also help the audio transcriber identify the individual voices on the cassette, though it also may have the disadvantage of making some group members rather self-conscious. In placing the cassette recorder care should also be taken to avoid adjacent extraneous noise. Bloor still ruefully recalls long sections of a group recording made in a private household being rendered useless by the house's dog coming into the room and repeatedly cracking a bone beside the recorder.

As was mentioned in Chapter 1, it is the systematic analysis of transcripts of audio recordings that distinguishes the use of focus groups in academic research from their use in commercial market research. In the latter, audio recording is mainly undertaken for quality control purposes and as a demonstration to the client that the groups contracted for have all actually taken place; analysis is based on the facilitator's reports or on an oral debriefing of the facilitator(s) by a report writer. There are two main advantages of using audio recordings and transcription as a basis for one's analysis. Firstly, and obviously, there is no need for a second person to manually record the interaction alongside the facilitator. Since their recording function has become redundant, this has encouraged researchers to learn and develop the specialist skills of the group facilitator. And the second advantage of basing the analysis on audio recordings and transcription is that it avoids the pitfalls of inaccurate and selective manual recording and inaccurate and selective recall by the facilitator. The topic of the analysis of transcripts is dealt with at length in Chapter 4.

Focusing exercises

In the introduction we distinguished focus groups from group interviews. In group interviews, the group is asked a sequence of predetermined questions, just as if the interviewer were speaking to a single interviewee: the group format is simply a matter of convenience and/or economy and the objective is to elicit the group's answers to those questions. Group interviews are rarely to be preferred to individual interviews in academic social research as individual differences in viewpoint within the group will be blurred and under-reported. In focus groups, pre-determined questions may also be asked, but the objective is not primarily to elicit the group's answers but rather to stimulate discussion and thereby understand (through subsequent analysis) the meanings and norms which underlie those group answers. In group interviews the interviewer seeks answers, in focus groups the facilitator seeks group interaction.

The focus group facilitator's questions are thus a 'focusing exercise', an attempt to concentrate the group's attention and interaction on a particular topic. The exercise need not, and frequently does not, take the form of a question, instead the group may be required to perform a specific task, hence the term 'focusing exercise'. One commonly used type of focusing exercise is a *ranking exercise*: the group is offered a list of statements and asked to agree among themselves a ranking of the statements in order of importance. In Box 3.1 we see a focusing exercise recently undertaken by Bloor as part of an ongoing study (being led by Lane, Kahveci and Sampson) of multicultural crewing in the global shipping industry: the two ranking exercises were each completed by a group of West African crewmen and a group of British merchant officers, all of them aboard a merchant vessel sailing under a flag of convenience and with each group having a different contractual status. The different statements were placed on different cards and the facilitator would place and re-place the cards in a different order across the table, depending on how the discussion about the relative importance of each proceeded. In such exercises, the different groups will commonly produce some differences in rankings. But more importantly, the discussion about the rankings serves to illustrate the deep differences (along with some important similarities) in the tacit understandings of each different group.

The instrumental purpose of such ranking exercises can be seen even more clearly in one of the exercises used by Kitzinger and her colleagues in their focus group investigations of public understandings of media messages on HIV/AIDS (Kitzinger, 1994a). The exercise consisted of a series of cards describing different groups of people (male homosexuals – that is, gays, doctors and nurses who treat people who have AIDS, people who have sex with many different partners of the opposite sex, and people who donate blood at a blood donor centre) and the groups were asked to rank each according to how much the people described on the cards were at risk of HIV/AIDS – 'greatly at risk', 'quite a lot at risk', 'not very much at risk', and 'not at all at risk'. None of the cards described actual risk practices for HIV (for example, the cards did not specify whether the male homosexuals undertook anal sex, and if so whether it was with or without a condom and whether or not it was part of a monogamous relationship), so a technical judgement of degree of risk, based on epidemiological evidence, could not be undertaken. But this spurious ranking exercise instrumentally served a different purpose, to lay bare the background assumptions that underlay the group's

BOX 3.1   FOCUSING EXERCISE ON MULTICULTURAL CREWING IN THE GLOBAL SHIPPING INDUSTRY

Exercise I
In a global shipping industry where crews may be made up of different nationalities and officers may be made up of different nationalities, what are the best things about the job as far as you are concerned?
Rank the following statements in order of importance:

a)   It is an opportunity to meet and talk to seafarers from different cultures.
b)   Multicultural crewing is the future of the shipping industry and we should not be afraid of change.
c)   It is a chance to learn new languages and to try different foods.
d)   It is a chance for seafarers from countries without merchant ships to get job opportunities.
e)   It is a chance for seafarers from countries without merchant ships to learn new skills.

Exercise II
. . . And what are the worst things about the job as far as you are concerned?

a)   Seafarers of one nationality are thrown out of work when they are replaced by other nationalities.
b)   Different nationalities get different pay for doing the same job.
c)   Different nationalities get different types of contracts – some get permanent contracts, some get temporary contracts.
d)   Difficulties in communication between different nationalities affect safety.
e)   Different nationalities keep to themselves and there is no feeling of being one community together on board ship.
f)   There are arguments because no-one likes the same food.
g)   Having different nationalities together leads to racial discrimination and racist abuse.

responses: Kitzinger pointed out that many of the group members in that study unquestioningly assumed that people were at risk of HIV as a consequence of their membership of 'risk groups' rather than through particular risk behaviours, and that people who were members of risk groups would naturally undertake certain risk behaviours (Kitzinger, 1994a: 164).

Box 3.2 illustrates a different kind of focusing exercise to a ranking exercise, namely that of the 'vignette'. Vignettes are hypothetical cases or scenarios with particular features which make them suggestive of real life situations to respondents, who are then asked what course of action

BOX 3.2   FOCUSING EXERCISE ON THE HEALTH BELIEFS OF
UK CHINESE CITIZENS

Card 1:   Woman aged 25. Waking unusually early in the morning.
          Crying without any apparent reason. Loss of appetite.
Card 2:   Three-month old baby. Vomiting, diarrhoea, high temperature.
Card 3:   Woman aged 65. Runny nose, slight temperature.
Card 4:   Man aged 45. Dizziness. Headaches. Blurred vision.
Card 5:   Female 50. Lumps evident in breast. Otherwise well.
Card 6:   Male 50. Lumps evident in upper chest. Otherwise well.

In the case of each of the persons described on the cards, does the person
need help? If so, where might the person get appropriate help? And what
kind of help might be useful?

should follow. They are commonly used in both surveys (for example, West, 1982) and qualitative interviewing (for example, Hughes, 1998) and, as was mentioned in Chapter 1, pre-pilot focus groups may even be used to supply the 'real life' anecdotal raw material for the construction of vignettes. The vignettes constructed by Prior et al. (forthcoming) and reproduced in Box 3.2 are deliberately rather more truncated and ambiguous than the vignettes usually used in survey research. In focus groups vignettes like those in Box 3.2 are often intended to be unclear and problematic; their very vagueness may act as a stimulus to the discussion. These vignettes were used in a series of focus groups on the health beliefs of the UK Chinese community, undertaken as preparatory work to a major national survey of the health behaviour of UK ethnic minorities. All the groups were facilitated by a Cantonese-speaker (in the co-presence of the senior researcher) and the vignettes are translated here from the Cantonese. It was notable that the vagueness of the vignettes served to highlight inter-group differences. Thus, the groups of Chinese men reacted with jokes and puzzlement to Vignette No.1 ('Woman aged 25. Waking unusually early in the morning. Crying without any apparent reason. Loss of appetite'), whereas the groups of Chinese women immediately recognized and empathized with the scenario, often equating the vignette with the clinical symptoms of depression, and to episodes in their own past life (Prior et al., forthcoming).

A third type of focusing exercise is the *news bulletin* exercise. This exercise was developed in studies of audience responses to media messages (Philo, 1990), but has wider potential applications. The exercise consists of the distribution to the group of a series of still photographs and a request to the group to use the photographs to compile their own news bulletin on a given topic (an enjoyable exercise for an extrovert group). Thus, in Kitzinger and her colleagues' study of audiences' reactions to HIV/AIDS media messages, the groups were given a series of deliberately decontextualized photographs (of a crowded city street, of a black patient in a hospital bed, of a mother with her baby, etc.) and asked to produce a news bulletin on AIDS (Kitzinger, 1993). The news bulletin exercise is often the occasion for some hilarity: in the HIV/AIDS study groups would sometimes mimic the format of the then-popular ITN news programme 'News at Ten', beginning with the strokes of Big Ben. Such kidding around is, of course, a good way to promote the coherence of the group.

Related to the news bulletin exercise, groups may be shown some photographs and asked to describe what they think is going on in the photograph. For example, in Thomas' focus groups, her returned holidaymakers were shown photographs clipped from travel brochures (a couple walking hand-in-hand down an empty beach at sunset, a couple talking in a hotel bar, etc.) and asked to describe what was going on in the photograph (had the couple in the bar just met or were they partners? etc.). In both the news bulletin and the brochure photographs, the stills were simply props to help groups to elaborate their background understandings of the research subject. (Were ordinary people in the street at risk of HIV/AIDS? How do unattached people of the opposite sex meet when on holiday?) And the interest for the researcher is as much or more in the discussion around the photographs as in their eventual consensual interpretation, or in their use in the spoof news bulletin.

These four types of focusing exercises – the ranking exercise, vignettes, the news bulletin, and photo interpretations – do not exhaust the possible range of focusing exercises, and researchers should always give careful thought to the selection and design of their own exercise, tailored to the research topic in question. The chosen design could be an adaptation of one of those types already outlined, or it could be an entirely idiosyncratic exercise. Or (better still) it could be both, in that the best designed focus groups probably incorporate two exercises. Dual exercise groups are to be preferred, first and foremost, because they allow the facilitator a second bite at the cherry. If the response of the group to the first exercise is somewhat muted, if the group is slow to cohere, then the introduction of a second exercise may revive flagging interest and give the group a new lease of life. The fail-safe character of dual exercise designs can be seen most clearly in designs which begin with a more open and exploratory exercise and then go onto a more structured exercise which re-covers some of the same ground as the first exercise. So, for example, a workgroup may be asked initially 'How has the job changed in the last ten years?' and the second exercise may be a ranking exercise where the group members are asked to rank in importance a number of ways in which their job has changed, with different pre-prepared cards for a number of ways in which the job has changed, plus a few blank cards to allow factoring in the ranking of changes mentioned in the first exercise but not anticipated in the prior construction of the cards. However, another reason for dual exercise designs (beyond the fail-safe factor) is to facilitate a *balanced*, multi-faceted coverage of the research topic, with one exercise pursuing positive aspects and a second exercise pursuing negative aspects of the issue in question. The dual ranking exercise in Box 3.1 is a design of this type.

The introduction of open-ended questions (such as 'How has the job changed in the past ten years?') raises the issue of whether focusing exercises should be used at all in focus groups. Shouldn't a skilful facilitator be able to ensure that a group addresses a given topic in adequate detail, without recourse to a focusing exercise? Is the use of focusing exercises simply a throwback to the early days of focus groups in market research, where a new product might be itself the 'focusing exercise' and the group would be asked to smell a new perfume or taste a new TV dinner and discuss their reactions? In effect, these are questions about the amount of structure that should be built into focus groups, one of the central issues in academic writings on focus groups (see the work of David Morgan, especially 1992, 1997, 1998; Morgan and Spanish, 1984). If too much structure is introduced, then the central advantage of focus groups (access to group interaction) is lost, as group members concentrate on responding to the questions of the facilitator, and the focus group is transformed into a mere group interview. The trick, of course, is to introduce sufficient structure to ensure that the group continues to address the research topic while not inhibiting the natural flow of group interaction. That is why task-setting, the setting of focusing exercises for the group, is a preferred research strategy, in that (ideally) it gives impetus to group interaction (albeit in a given direction) rather than restricting it.

There are a number of other advantages associated with the use of focusing exercises. One is that the 'props' of the exercise (the printed cards or the still photographs lying on the table) are themselves a convenient reminder of the group's task and thus a silent guard against straying into irrelevancies. But a more important advantage lies in the fact that the task is itself something of an ice-breaker: it allows group members to treat the occasion in a business-like manner and lose any initial self-consciousness in the task-at-hand. For the self-conscious group member, embarking on the focusing exercise has the same effect as reaching for a cigarette used to have after entering a crowded room (before smoking in public places became socially unacceptable). Another considerable advantage of focusing exercises is that they ease the task of analysis in that they facilitate comparisons across the different groups (see Chapter 4). Where comparisons between groups are more straightforward and more numerous, then fewer groups in total may need to be run in order to answer the research question.

Thus it is clear that some kind of focusing exercise is always to be preferred. However, it will have been noticed that some focusing exercises are themselves more structured than others. The news bulletin exercise is more structured than a question such as 'How has the job changed in the last ten years?'. So, in designing the focus group exercises, a decision has to be made about the degree of structure to be preferred in the exercise. This decision will turn on the nature of the research question: some research questions will require a more exploratory approach than others (see Chapter 1). As a general rule, where the objective of the groups is to generate raw materials for a later, more quantitative study (the collection of narratives to form the basis for subsequent survey vignettes, for example, or the accumulation of examples of group vocabulary for a future taxonomy of terms), then more open-ended exercises may be preferred. For many other research questions, researchers may prefer the more prudent approach of preparing one more exploratory and one more structured exercise.

It will be appreciated that final decisions on the nature and content of the focusing exercises should be made on the basis of piloting. Pilot work is only superfluous where the focus groups are part of a multi-methods research design (see Chapter 1) and other methods in the design can serve as pilot materials for the focus groups. Thus, the materials for the focus groups in the multicultural crewing study in Box 3.1 were derived from earlier depth interviews. Pilot work might involve using a shortlist of draft exercises and finally modifying and selecting the two most effective. The question 'How has the job changed in the last ten years?' is likely to be bathetic and lead to premature closure when asked of a group of workers who have just switched to, say, computerized systems or teleworking. But the question 'How does the job compare with that of ten years ago?' might serve as good stimulus for discussion. The choice of focus group exercises should be an empirical decision, based on pilot evidence.

Facilitator or controller?

There is a story, told and re-told with different protagonists, about an unruly focus group who ignored and ridiculed the young researcher: she had lost control, a matter for subsequent tears and self-recriminations; but when she steeled herself to listen the tape, she was surprised at how much valuable, usable material the tape contained. The moral of the tale is that the facilitator of a focus group does not need, and should not seek, to control the group: sometimes the facilitator may emerge from a most successful group feeling that she has been holding a tiger by the tail for the last hour and a half. A facilitator should *facilitate* the group, not control it. Control is necessary for a successful group interview, as it is for depth interviews and survey work. But a facilitator who seeks to control certain focus groups may be doing the study a disservice: if the aim is to facilitate group interaction in such a way as to understand group norms and meanings, then the group interaction of certain groups may be distorted by too much external control. A group of football supporters or recreational drug users may interact characteristically in rather anarchic ways. If that characteristic ebullience is too much restrained, then the group itself may dissolve into a collection of muted and separated individuals. The focus group facilitator is not a marginal figure to the group, as an ethnographer might be. But the ideal relationship of the facilitator to her group members, is that of a background figure, not a foreground figure – the theatre manager rather than the director of the play.

It is commonplace for focus group facilitators in commercial market research to use flip charts or whiteboards to progress, consolidate and summarize group viewpoints. And at the end of the group, the flipchart or board can serve as an *aide-memoire* for the facilitator's report or their briefing to the report writer. But it is arguable that the use of flipcharts and whiteboards is counter-productive in academic focus group research. The cassette recorder is already in place to record events and the overt summarizer role of the flipchart operative places the facilitator too much at the centre of the group interaction. Standing beside the board or flipchart, in the eye of all the seated group members, the facilitator is too much in the foreground rather than the background – too much the director, rather than the theatre manager.

Just as the facilitator must avoid leading the group, so the facilitator must also seek to avoid the over-domination of the group by particular individual members. In part, this is a matter of group composition, composing groups which do not contain within them persons of both superordinate and subordinate statuses. But in part too, it is a matter of skilful facilitation. At the outset (and reiterated where necessary), it is valuable to 'validate the expression of differences' (Morgan, 1992: 185), to state that the researchers want to hear about a range of experiences and if members disagree with a voiced viewpoint, then it is important for them to make their disagreement known. Similarly, if one member makes a suggestion but there are no spontaneous murmurs of agreement from the other members, then the facilitator should check that the suggestion does in fact chime with others views. This checking is most easily accomplished in an exercise like the ranking exercise, where the facilitator herself may be the person arranging the separate pieces of card in rank order down the table, and so checking with all parties on the correct placement of the cards appears merely common courtesy.

Relatedly, the facilitator must not just avoid domination of the group by individual members, but must also seek to encourage contributions from the more timorous. This should not be read as an injunction to play the part of party hostess. As a callow young researcher, Bloor once found himself at a Medical Research Council lunch at the same table as the formidable Dame Margarita Laski: noting the general high table tenor of the conversation, Bloor decided to devote himself exclusively to his food, but Dame Margarita would have it otherwise and eventually addressed him directly with the devastating question, 'What is your favourite cathedral?'. Such heavy-handed invitations to participate are likely to be counter-productive, but less threatening invitations can be issued, by attending to non-verbal cues, for example: 'You're nodding Bill, do you agree with what Ben said then?'. It is important also to make it clear at the outset that there are no 'correct' answers to the ranking exercise, the photo interpretation exercise, or whatever. Group members should not be inhibited by uncertainties about their abilities to formulate 'correct' answers (and should be discouraged from formulating answers that they think the facilitator might approve of) by the previously-mentioned validation of the expression of differences, stressing the wish to hear a range of different viewpoints.

Where groups are composed of members drawn from pre-existing social groups, it is both inevitable and desirable that the group inter-actions in the focus group reflect the group interactions in the pre-existing group: one group member may be more forceful than others, another may be the group humorist, and so on. Of course, the facilitator should not seek to overturn these natural features of group interaction: if the objective is to obtain information on group meanings, processes and norms, then it is clearly a mistake to attempt to alter substantially the character of the group. Nevertheless, all group life possesses some vari-ability and fluidity on which a skilled facilitator can build, in order to ensure that 'the quiet one' makes a relatively more substantial contri-bution, and so on. In particular, the facilitator should ensure that the group does not fractionate into different simultaneous conversations. But it should always be remembered that the focus group is meant to be tapping into group life, not changing it.

The deathly hush: group silences

Possibly the greatest anxiety for focus group facilitators, once their group has actually arrived, is that no-one will say anything. Using silence is a well-documented prompt in interviewing (drawing out further comment from the interviewee), but it is a dangerous and usually counter-productive tool for facilitators of focus groups. In group situ-ations, after a certain amount of time has passed, breaking a silence can be more awkward or socially embarrassing than the continued silence. Pugsley (1996) sensed there was some shared guilty knowledge among the pupils in one of her focus groups, which articulated itself as an impenetrable silence. In Robson's recent focus group work with dentists there appeared to be a reluctance to break ranks within a group of peers all working in the same area in the same kind of conditions: critical appraisal of common practices may smack of group disloyalty. Often there are conditions within groups that foster an unwillingness to discuss certain issues with each other.

As well as discussion being stifled by suspicion of each other, focus group participants may also be restrained by a sense of suspicion of the researcher or facilitator. In Robson's (2000) focus groups with dental patients, all of the groups sought to establish whether she was herself a dentist, all then expressing relief at then being able to be 'open' when discovering she was not. Conversely, focus groups with dentists in the same project (Robson, 1999) required her to overcome their suspicion of her as a non-dentist undertaking a study of their practices on behalf of the health authority for which they worked.

Sometimes group silences may be a consequence of problems in the recruitment process. Despite all attempts by the researcher to ensure informed consent, low status groups (such as schoolchildren or third world peasant communities) may not always feel free to refuse to participate in groups organized by a high status (white adult) researcher. Such recruitment difficulties may be exacerbated if recruitment has occurred via a superordinate gate-keeper, such as a teacher. In such circumstances, silence (or worse – a limping discussion of bland super-ficialities) may be a legitimate and effective group weapon. Foucault has written extensively on power relationships and the exercise of super-ordinate power through techniques of surveillance (see especially Foucault, 1980). All power, as Foucault recognized, provokes counter-vailing resistance and the most successful technique of subordinate resistance is concealment (Bloor and McIntosh, 1989). Where silences are a consequence of recruitment problems, then the remedy lies in the recruitment process, not in more skilful facilitation.

Relatedly, silences can occur because of the composition of the group. There may be a pre-existing hostility or suspicion between some or all the group members which may inhibit frank discussion. Or, in a group containing persons of different statuses, those of subordinate status may feel it is inappropriate or ill-advised to comment on a given topic, deferring to the opinion of a superordinate group member. So discussion is curtailed and silence is misread as concurrence. Again, the remedy for this lies in the different composition of groups (see Chapter 2), not in particular techniques of facilitation. Furthermore, silence in these cir-cumstances may be preferable to the broaching of pre-existing hostility. While it is unlikely that a focus group will ever degenerate into some-thing akin to a Jerry Springer show, it is important to be on guard for anything said or done that may affect participants either individually or in their relationships with others. While the apparently shared guilty knowledge in Pugsley's focus groups was intriguing to the researchers, they would not have wished for the pupils to have aired this information given that their relationships as a year group continued well beyond their hour in the focus group. If discussions do get too heated, the researcher should make efforts to calm participants down, breaking the discussion for a while if necessary (see the section on debriefing later in this chapter). While it is acceptable for participants to leave challenged, researchers should not let participants leave unduly distressed by the experience. If strong opinion and disagreement might reasonably be expected for a given topic, moderators should lay down 'ground rules' at the start of the discussion requesting participants to respect others' views (Kreuger, 1998).

When focus group participants aren't talking as much as the researcher had hoped, or are talking about issues 'off topic', there is a danger that in encouraging speech, or refocusing the group, the facilitator instigates a 'question and answer' pattern in the group. A number of tactics can help avoid this. The physical arrangement of the group should suggest the facilitator is part of the group, but their positioning should not create a focal point for comments to be directed at. A long rectangular table or seating arrangement, with the facilitator alone at one end encourages answers to be directed down to them rather than around the group. Having a focusing exercise is a necessary aid for facilitators, but if presented as questions rather than issues, they can lead the nervous facilitator to recite them verbatim rather than incorporating them on the hoof into the discussion at hand. Sliding into a group interview format may result from the participants' eagerness to be asked questions. If they are not familiar with focus groups, they may expect to be asked questions, and that they should direct answers to the facilitator. It may not necessarily be the case that they cannot or do not want to discuss with each other, but simply that they are unfamiliar with the rules of engagement. So it may be worthwhile to reiterate those opening remarks about the 'validation of the expression of differences' and the wish to hear about a range of views and experiences. If, despite this, the initial focusing exercise fails to stimulate more than a limping discussion, then it may be best to cut one's losses and move quickly onto a second focusing exercise, before a pattern of embarrassing silences becomes firmly implanted.

As was mentioned in the previous discussion of the facilitator role, there are small host/hostess-like courtesies which the facilitator can perform to help the discussion along, such as attending to and commenting on non-verbal cues ('Jill, you're looking as if you're disagreeing with Jack?'). But it is a mistake to think that the facilitation of focus groups is some esoteric craft skill which can be performed only by the Oprah Winfreys of this world, or by some highly paid specialist consultant with flashing teeth and flipchart. Obviously, some researchers will have better social and group skills than others, but it is our contention that anyone can operate moderately successful focus groups if they give sufficient prior consideration to issues such as recruitment, composition, venue and focusing exercises. Successful focus groups are a matter of planning rather than personality. And not everyone is attracted to flashing teeth in any case.

Length and payment

These two issues are best addressed together, since when participation is paid the facilitator may legitimately suggest a longer period of attendance, provided the fee is sufficiently remunerative. But when no fee is paid, it is surely discourteous to take up to two hours of members' time. If the agreed timeslot is to be less than two hours and time is to be found within that period for the completion of a pre-group questionnaire and for the post-group debriefing (see below), then the group itself should not run for longer than a hour and a half. Even if the group is going very well and the group members appear enthusiastic, the facilitator should wind things up after 90 minutes. At all costs, the facilitator should avoid the premature departure of some group members, altering the composition and dynamics of the group; such premature departures will be increasingly likely as time goes on.

The venues for some settings may themselves dictate the amount of time available – the room booking slots in a community centre, the school timetable, the period set aside for a workplace meeting, and so forth. Over-running these timeslots will make the researcher very unpopular and may even threaten the continuity of the study. One of the first considerations in any pilot work must therefore be the likely running time required to complete the planned focusing exercises. Of course, two different groups can take very different amounts of time to complete the same exercises, but nevertheless the facilitator must develop a rough grasp from pilot work of the minimum amount of time required to address the planned exercises in a satisfactory fashion. If that satisfactory minimum is more than an hour, then the groups should perhaps be redesigned to allow a shorter completion time.

To these strictures on timing it may be objected that, other things being equal, where two groups are addressing the same exercises, the group that takes longer will generally furnish the better data, and that an early finish to a group often indicates inhibited group interaction and premature group closure. The truth of the objection is admitted, but one can have too much of a good thing and imposing on people's limited free time may be too high a price to pay for additional high quality data.

The convention of paying a fee to focus group members probably stems from focus groups' commercial history in market research, where the fee offered by market researchers is a considerable aid to recruitment, especially among the young and disadvantaged. Against the convention of offering a fee to attenders in academic focus group research, it may be objected that ethnographies and depth interviews may also cut deeply into research subjects' free time, but no fee is sought or offered. However, focus group members may also incur additional expenses not incurred by participation in studies using other methods – transport costs to the venue, possible loss of earnings, the possible need to make child care arrangements, etc. So the attendance fee for group members in academic social research is generally termed an 'attendance allowance for out-of-pocket expenses' and is currently around £15 to £25 per person in the UK (say around $25 to $40). This is a large enough sum to be an incentive to attend for the disadvantaged, but not for the better off. So it has become commonplace for studies requiring better off participants to offer considerably larger allowances, although it is said that allowances of £50 and even £100 are still insufficient to attract more than a fraction of some target groups of professionals, such as General Practitioners or Dentists. The cost of members' attendance allowances, together with the cost of audiotranscription (see Chapter 4) and the difficulty of scheduling an appropriate time that all may attend, has made virtual focus groups an increasingly attractive alternative to 'live' focus groups for studies involving professionals with Internet access (see Chapter 5).

Of course, there will be circumstances where payment is inappropriate: attenders of 'feedback' focus groups, for example, will have an entirely non-pecuniary motivation, and focus groups scheduled in work-time or school time should also not involve payment. Where focus groups are conducted as part of post-graduate studies, payment will not normally be possible, and where the research is funded by a charity, payment may not be appropriate. But focus groups should not be discounted as a possible method in such circumstances. It may nevertheless be possible to offer thanks in kind (tea and biscuits, the offer of a lift home) and many potential participants will have motivations to participate in academic research (altruism, a commitment to the research topic, a commitment to the researcher, curiosity) which render considerations of expense and remuneration inconsequential.

The payment issue is particularly thorny in the use of focus groups in participative research designs. Funding will always be insufficient to pay group members and/or indigenous facilitators at the same salaries as the researcher, even on a pro rata basis, but different scales of remuneration may undermine aspirations to egalitarian co-participation. Since participative designs are most common in research among the deprived and disadvantaged, payment issues can be a source of considerable tension and (more commonly) guilt. However, with the pragmatism of the poor, disadvantaged research participants are always likely to prefer half a loaf to none at all.

Debriefing

All group members should have the opportunity to be debriefed on their experience – a further reason why over-running and early departures should be avoided. The completion of post-group questionnaires provides an opportunity for individual debriefings, but on balance pre-group questionnaires are to be preferred (see above). Some opportunity for private individual chat is provided by asking members to sign receipts for their attendance allowances.

Most members of most groups will have no more need of a private chat with the researcher than a parishioner would need a chat with the minister at the end of a Sunday service, but there will be an occasional need for a private word and the researcher should be alert to this possibility and react appropriately. An appropriate reaction might be to suggest that the group member stay behind for a minute after the others have gone, or to arrange to drop off that member last, or to arrange to phone the member that evening or the next day. In most instances where a group member seeks a private word, it will be no greater matter than an additional question or two about the purpose of the research, or the reporting of the research, or the confidentiality of the research: what was, before the group, perhaps a matter of limited interest to the member, has now become a more salient issue and more information may be sought. For this reason, it may be good practice to end the focus group with a short recapitulation on the use to which the transcript will be put, the confidentiality of the data, the wiping of the tape, the publication of the results, and so forth, thus reducing the need for any private enquiries on such topics. Alternatively, that recapitulation could be reproduced on a short information sheet handed out at the end, which also invites interested members to phone a contact number if they have further enquiries.

Very occasionally a focus group member may become upset. Emphatically, this should not be dealt with in the group: focus groups are constituted for research purposes, not therapeutic purposes and well-intentioned meddling in therapeutic matters by untrained researchers and/or fellow group members could make matters worse. If a person becomes seriously upset, they should be taken out of the group (and the group left to its own devices for a bit). If the person appears less seriously troubled, then they can be debriefed privately at the end of the group. Once more, no therapeutic work should be attempted: just tea, sympathy and the offer of a lift or a taxi home. If necessary, the researcher might make further enquiries and phone back the next day with an appropriate contact number for professional help; the Citizens Advice Bureau may be able to suggest a contact number if the researcher is stumped.

Where groups are constituted from pre-existing social groups there is a slight danger of a group member making a disclosure which could damage their reputation among some fellow-group members (say, the disclosure of an abortion or a previous conviction). If such disclosures are being signalled in advance, then the facilitator should immediately change the conversation and attempt to head the disclosure off. Focus groups are not therapeutic groups and neither are they for the confession of sins. If the disclosure cannot be headed off, then it should be responded to only briefly and in a business-like way in the group, reminding members that the group's deliberations should be treated as confidential. The disclosure should then be responded to privately and at greater length at the end of the group. Again, no therapeutic work should be attempted.

On balance and over time, it is probable that the researcher will actually feel more trauma and remorse than the group member who has made the damaging disclosure; the researcher may wish to talk the matter over with a senior colleague or with another suitable counsellor. If it were appropriate to pass any comment at all on such matters in a methods textbook of this kind, it would be the consoling words of a senior psychiatrist with many years of group therapeutic practice behind him. Namely, that a confession that feels like a lion in the chest turns out to be more like a mouse to the patient when it is out in the open, and that ordinary members of the public (and focus group members) show more compassion and therapeutic sensibility than most psychiatrists give them credit for.

Whether or not the study in question is designed as overtly participative research and whether or not the focus groups in question are feedback groups, it may be thought common courtesy that, after taking part in the fairly arduous process of a focus group, one should offer participants a copy of the eventual research findings. Sadly, when the participants learn how far off is the day when those findings will be ready, then their polite interest tends to diminish. For those participants for whom the findings are simply a pleasure postponed, then a business card or an information sheet will furnish your address and telephone number for them to enquire about the results in due course.

Conclusion

The main consideration in the choice of venue should be the possible impact of the venue on recruitment, considerations of convenience and accessibility should be paramount. Where pre-existing social groups are being recruited (such as a school peer group), then the ideal venue will be in the natural social setting of the group (such as the school). Unless a focus group has been recruited as a sub-group of a wider study group, it will be necessary at some point to collect some background socio-demographic data on group members and it may be desirable also to check for initial individual differences in viewpoint on the focus group topic. These two functions can be combined in a pre-group self-completion questionnaire. Focusing exercises are an attempt to concentrate the groups attention on a particular topic (without reversion to a question-and-answer group interview format) by requiring the group to undertake a group task which requires the group to interact on the study topic. Popular focusing exercises are ranking exercises, vignettes, the news bulletin, and photo interpretation. Control of the group by the facilitator is unnecessary and may be counter-productive (a degree of disruption may even be a natural feature of the interaction of the group in question), but the facilitator should attempt to ensure that a full range of viewpoints are raised within the group. Where group members receive no payment, then it seems discourteous for the event to last as long as two hours, but it is commonplace for focus group members to receive an 'attendance allowance' and under these circumstances longer groups may be more acceptable. There should always be a conversational opportunity for group participants to ask private questions at the end of the group and an information sheet should be available with a contact number for requesting more information or a copy of the eventual end-of-grant report. Above all, successful focus groups require careful preparation and planning. One is reminded of Churchill's famous remark about the notice and preparation he required for an 'extemporary' speech: focus groups are naturalistic rather than natural events and cannot and should not be left to chance and circumstance; their naturalism has to be carefully contrived by the researcher.

EXERCISES

1   Design two focusing exercises suitable for an exploratory study of why drivers may break the law. Explain the reasons for your choices.
2   Your focus groups on deviant driving comprise the following different groups: truck drivers from different companies, commercial representatives from the same company, offenders serving community service orders, retired police officers, attenders at an evening keep-fit class, day-release students, mothers picking up their children from a school, office cleaners, teenagers hanging about outside a chip shop, and members of a rugby club. Suggest a suitable venue for each group and explain the reasons for your choices.
3   Compare and contrast the roles of focus group facilitator and depth interviewer.

4

Analysis

CONTENTS

The data that focus group discussions produce are distinct in a number of ways from data collected by other qualitative methods. As has been stated throughout this book, the aim of the focus group is to initiate discussion between group members, and it is this interaction that makes the data distinct. Kitzinger (1994a) best describes the seemingly chaotic nature of focus group data, drawing on a study of AIDS media messages. She tells how participants brainstormed, argued, misunderstood, interrupted, and ridiculed each other. They used a variety of methods to put their message across, including singing, and acting out. This interactive effect results in data which may include instances where people talk at once, where sentences remain unfinished, where people go on to contradict themselves and others, where people's arguments develop as they discuss the topic with others, and where people misinterpret other's comments and take the discussion off in another direction. This, and the overwhelming quantity of data that can be collected by this method (a 90-minute focus group can generate more than 100 pages of transcript) can leave any researcher wondering where to start with analysis.

A variety of approaches can be taken to the analysis of qualitative data (see for example Coffey and Atkinson, 1996), and the analysis of focus group data should evidently draw on these established methods. Analysis can for instance take a conversation analytic approach (see for example Myers, 1998 and Myers and Macnaghten, 1999), can concentrate on group dynamics (Kitzinger and Farquhar, 1999) or, as in this chapter, can concentrate on providing an understanding of substantive issues in the data.

Two approaches to the analysis of substantive content, namely analytic induction and logical analysis, provide systematic processes, or step-by-step procedures to achieving rigorous analysis. It is through reflection on the use of these two methods that this chapter will illustrate that the distinct nature of focus group data raises particular problems for analysis. The chapter will show how it is necessary to keep in mind the dynamics of the data and the form of speech collected in a group situation when considering the whole process of analysis, from transcription requirements to interpretation of the data.

Transcription of focus group data

> There cannot be a *perfect* transcript of a tape-recording. Everything depends upon what you are trying to do in the analysis, as well as upon practical considerations involving time and resources. (Silverman, 1993: 124)

The requirements of transcription of focus group data for substantive analysis are something that go largely unmentioned, and the significance of transcription is therefore perhaps underestimated. Decisions do need to be made by the researcher about what is a suitable level of transcription for analysis purposes. Krueger (1994) states that transcription is not always necessary, and that in some cases analysis can be carried out on the basis of listening to but not transcribing tapes, or on the notes or the memory of the moderator. This cannot be satisfactory for academic research. Attempts at analysis without transcription will lead to loss of much of the richness of the data and will risk a selective and superficial analysis. In order for a detailed and rigorous analysis to be conducted, a thorough transcription of the tape recording of the focus group is required.

Much of what can be read about the conventions of transcription originates from conversation or discourse analysis (Hammersley and Atkinson, 1995; Silverman, 1993). However, as the focus of these methods of analysis is on the actual talk, these conventions are particularly rigorous, and include such things as the timing of pauses in speech. For a detailed substantive analysis, some of the conventions used in conversation and discourse analysis are useful, whereas other aspects can be dropped (see below).

All transcription is time consuming. It has, for instance, been estimated that transcribing time is often at least five times the recorded time

(Hammersley and Atkinson, 1995). The nature of the focus group data – the fact that a number of people are involved in the speech – makes the transcription of focus groups more complex than transcription of data collected by other qualitative methods. A one-to-one interview, for example, evidently involves only two speakers, who are thus easily identifiable, and who rarely create interruptions, nor talk at the same time as each other. Focus group data, involving group interaction, are more complex. One hour of taped focus group may take 8 hours to transcribe and can lead to 100 pages of text.

There are a number of points to be adhered to in transcription of focus group data. First, every effort should be made to transcribe *all* recorded speech. This includes: *all* speakers, where more than one person is talking, not just the dominant voice; all unfinished and interrupted speech; very brief extracts of speech, such as agreement with the main speaker, in the form of 'mm' or 'yeah'. Where speech is inaudible, and this may be the case perhaps because of the accent of the speaker or because people are talking at once, then it is necessary to transcribe as much of the speech as is possible, to provide suggested interpretations where useful and, if no interpretation can be made, to note that a section of the data is missing. (The group moderator may be the person best placed, due to memory of the group, to clear up any uncertainties in what was said).

Second, as mentioned above, people do not speak in neat planned sentences. They repeat themselves, hesitate or pause, say 'um' and 'er', and go off track. Speech should be transcribed as it occurs and not 'tidied up' (see also section on reporting of speech). Third, in addition to the content of the speech, other oral communication, such as laughter needs to be noted. There may also be instances where body movement/language is crucial to the reading of the transcript. Kitzinger (1994a: 166–167), for example, describes how participants in a series of focus groups exploring people's understanding of AIDS media messages 'acted out the "look of an AIDS carrier" (contorting their faces, squinting and shaking)'.

Finally, it is necessary as far as possible to identify the speaker. A useful tool here, and also to set people at their ease, is to ask each member of the group, as the first group exercise, to say their name and then a few sentences about themselves or about a non-threatening topic. This can then serve as a reference point for transcription – you have a piece of speech from each participant to use as a basis for identification. In addition, the group moderator should make use of participant's names where possible, such as in 'Thank you Sarah.' and 'Dave, you mentioned . . .', thus providing reference points for the identification of a speaker throughout the tape. If a second moderator is used and is involved in note taking then identification of a speaker may be one of their roles. The group moderator may be best placed to confirm speakers, as they may hold a picture in their head of the person the voice belongs to, and are likely to remember at least some of what was said by whom (this is obviously more likely the sooner the transcription is completed, and certainly before another group is conducted). The speaker can also in some instances be confirmed by things they say. Speaker identification is not however always possible, particularly with short extracts of speech or where the speaker merely agrees with what has just been said. If there is doubt about identification then speech should be marked as unidentified (but including gender if relevant).

As mentioned earlier, the accepted methods for transcribing text have been developed largely for the purposes of conversation and discourse analysis (Hammersley and Atkinson, 1995; Silverman, 1993). These are listed in a detailed appendix by Atkinson and Heritage (1984), and are drawn on by Silverman (1993) and Myers (1998) in their suggestions of useful notation. The requirements for a substantive analysis are not as rigorous as these authors propose (Myers and Macnaghten (1999) state that a full transcript for conversation analysis purposes takes four times longer than producing text as readable prose). What can be dropped from conversational analysis requirements in particular is the timing of pauses (although pauses and hesitation should be noted as transcriber added text). The aspects which are important for transcription of focus groups plus their suggested notation are provided in Box 4.1, and an example of text using these conventions is provided below. The extract, from a study of adolescent smoking behaviour (Frankland and Bloor, 1999) is of pupils talking about the pressures they perceive in giving up smoking.

Sarah: [They'll try to stop them. [all talking at once here]
Jackie: [They'll try to stop
Unidentified: [( )
Karen: No miss[
Jackie: [They'll try to force her not to give up.
Karen: She'll try to give up, when she's trying to give up, but she'll be round all her friends who are smoking and she just won't be able to give up.
Unidentified: No
Karen: [She'll just
Jackie: [No, and she'll be gasping for a fag.
Karen: She'll just, yeah want a fag and she'll have to (book after) them, or take one off them or something, innit.

In summary, the transcript needs to reproduce as near as possible the group as it happened, so that anyone reading the transcript can really 'see' how the group went. Editing should certainly be kept to a bare minimum at transcription stage, an exact copy of the speech being required for analysis purposes. If any editing is required to render the text readable then it should be done at the reporting stage (see later section on reporting speech).

It can be helpful for the researcher responsible for analysis to do their own transcription, as this helps them become familiar with their data

---

BOX 4.1   TRANSCRIPTION REQUIREMENTS FOR SUBSTANTIVE ANALYSIS

[	to indicate the point at which the current speaker is overlapped by another's speech
(attempt)	suggestions regarding uncertain transcription
( )	unintelligible speech
–	speaker's emphasis
WORD	loud utterance
[ ]	transcriber added text, e.g. pause, sign, body movement, acting out

Source: Adapted from Silverman, 1993

---

and may also provide early thoughts for the analysis. (It may be useful to have a notepad next to the transcribing equipment in order to note down any thoughts as they occur.) With timings of research programmes, it is not however always possible nor desirable for the researcher to undertake all transcription. If a third party carries out the task, then the main researcher should brief the transcriber as to the requirements and notation of transcription. Most importantly, the researcher should listen to the tapes while reading the completed transcript, for purposes of familiarization and to check for quality and completeness. A good quality transcribing machine which incorporates an automatic backspace facility can save the transcriber a large amount of time. If the analyst is planning to use one of the computer packages that aid data handling (see later section on data storage and retrieval), then the required formatting can be undertaken at the time of transcription. Each package has its own requirements, which are generally straightforward.

Analysis

The analysis of qualitative data can be approached in various ways (see Coffey and Atkinson, 1996). Crucially, that analysis must be systematic and rigorous, reflecting the views of all cases, not, for instance, only those that fit the researcher's own agenda, or are the most interesting or the most commonly mentioned topics. This section will discuss the use of two approaches to qualitative analysis: analytic induction and logical analysis. These provide step-by-step methods, to achieve rigorous analysis. The purpose of presenting these methods is not to dictate that these are the only ways to approach the analysis of focus group data. The discussion aims to illustrate that, in the use of such methods, issues arise which are related to the nature of focus group data.

The section comprises three parts, discussing the stages of indexing, data storage and retrieval, and interpretation (although these stages do, of course, run consecutively). Discussion of these issues concentrates on their particular application to focus group data. Readers are referred for more detailed discussions to qualitative methods texts such as Coffey and Atkinson (1996), Hammersley and Atkinson (1995) and Silverman (1993).

Indexing

Many qualitative texts can be consulted for discussion of the process of indexing of qualitative data (see, for example, Coffey and Atkinson, 1996; Dey, 1993; Lofland and Lofland, 1995; Miles and Huberman, 1994). This section will provide a very brief overview of this stage of analysis and will discuss issues of particular relevance to focus group data.

Once transcription is complete, the analyst is faced with pages and pages of data to be analysed. The first step in this process is to index the data in order to make them manageable for interpretation. The aim of indexing is to bring together all extracts of data that are pertinent to a particular theme, topic or hypothesis (Coffey and Atkinson, 1996). If the analyst was also the focus group moderator and has transcribed at least some of the text, she/he will arrive at this stage with a fair knowledge of the data. The process of indexing then involves the analyst reading and re-reading the text and assigning index codes, which relate to the content of the data and are of interest to the researcher's analytic framework. At the start, index codes are likely to be quite broad, and to then become more narrow and focused as the work continues. The process can be likened to chapter headings and sub-headings (Frankland and Bloor, 1999). In a study of adolescent smoking behaviour (Frankland and Bloor, 1999) the focus of the analysis was on perceived pressures on quitting smoking. The index 'peer pressure' encompassed quite large sections of the text, as this was the focus of the sessions. Within this however, focus group participants talked of different types of peer pressure, such as bullying and exclusion from the group. These types of pressure would thus form subcategories of the index 'peer pressure'. Further analytical work showed that within the category 'exclusion' there was a distinction between 'real friends' who would not exclude, and people who 'use you for fags' who would. These indexes became subcategories of the index 'exclusion'.

The analyst should not be too worried at the indexing stage about the allocation of a particular index to a particular extract of data. The final setting of an index will come later at the interpretative stage, when the extract can be compared to other extracts which have been allocated the same index code. At this early stage, the analyst should work on including all possibly relevant data within an index code (Frankland and Bloor, 1999). As the analyst works progressively through each case, new

BOX 4.2   EXAMPLE OF INDEXED TEXT

Simon:

. . . you know, like some people don't pressure   peer pressure
people into smoking, people just if, say like, say
somebody was smoking and I was gonna give
up, I don't think these [indicating his friends]
would bully me, because they're like my   bullying
friends, aren't they, and they're not gonna just   type of friend
come up to me, punching me, 'you've stopped   exclusion
smoking so you're not my friend', are they?

index codes are likely to emerge. This necessitates returning to any previously indexed cases so that these can be included. The analyst can allocate several index labels to the same piece of text and can allocate indexes to extracts of text of different sizes, such as a sentence, a paragraph or a page of data. The extract of text given in Box 4.2 originates from Frankland and Bloor's (1999) study of adolescent smoking, and the group are talking about perceived pressures if someone gives up smoking. The paragraph has been assigned four different index codes. The index code 'peer pressure' relates to a larger section of text which encompasses this paragraph, while the other three codes relate directly to this extract.

There is a danger with the indexing and sorting method within qualitative analysis that the analyst becomes focused on small extracts of data and loses sight of where those data sit within the whole (Lofland and Lofland, 1995). This can be a particular issue with focus groups, again an artefact of the interactive nature of the data. A coded piece of data may contain a statement or view that was later contradicted or developed either by the original speaker or by other group members (Catterall and Maclaran, 1997; Myers, 1998). Catterall and Maclaran (1997) illustrate how a woman manager, participating in a focus group to discuss gender issues at work, developed her argument over the course of the group from being dismissive of gender issues to admitting that gender may have an impact on management for her own organization. Using a conversation analysis approach, Myers (1998) describes a section of a focus group where a participant raises 'this nuclear stuff' as an issue of concern for the future. He shows how other group members take this to mean nuclear weapons and how it takes the participant several minutes of focus group talk to state that in fact she was talking of waste from nuclear power. Myers states that:

The analyst who simply codes such an utterance, removing it from its context, would assign *this nuclear stuff* to one category or another – waste or weapons –

and would miss an important message of the passage, that for these people the two topics are intertwined. (Myers, 1998: 96)

These two examples therefore illustrate how it is necessary during the indexing of focus group data to ensure that the context of any speech extract is studied (and that the context can be easily returned to), looking at any one individual's speech over the course of the focus group and looking at how that speech fits into what other participants are saying (Catterall and Maclaran, 1997). It is at this stage that the unpicking of the data will take place: the analyst needs to work through the arguments of individuals as well as of the group in order to make sense of and be able to index separate passages of data. This illustrates also the importance of attempting to identify individual voices from within the group, so that changing points of view can be followed through the transcript.

Methods of data storage and retrieval

As has already been stated, indexing is a means of making data manageable for analysis purposes. The researcher requires a method of collecting together all extracts of text which have been allocated the same index, to be able to retrieve them for comparison with other extracts given the same index. This can be (and was in the past) done manually, using photocopies and an organized filing system, or a card index method. Using the former method the researcher physically places copies of each extract of indexed data into a folder along with all other extracts containing that index. With the card index method, the analyst marks indexes on a complete copy of data and then notes location data (such as interview number, page number, paragraph number) on a set of cards.

Today, there is an array of packages (such as Ethnograph, NUD•IST) which are designed to facilitate the analysis of qualitative data. All of these packages contain facilities for the storage and retrieval of text by researcher given codes (the computer does not do this, it only works on those codes that the researcher has previously entered). Some packages can do quite sophisticated retrievals based on the presence or absence of more than one code, and some allow for memos and socio-demographic data to be stored and searched alongside the data. Some of the packages go further than this and contain functions that can be used to construct and test theoretical propositions. For a discussion of the various packages and the sorts of functions they perform, see, for example, Richards and Richards, 1994.

The main benefit of these qualitative data packages is that they can retrieve all text about a particular code with ease and efficiency. However, the decision to use one of them is to a degree a matter of personal preference (how good one is at dealing with manual files, how well one can work with documents on a computer screen, for instance), and should take into account the amount of data and time and resources available. It may be the case that for small amounts of data, one of the manual methods are suitable.

Interpretation

The following section will describe two possible approaches to systematic analysis of qualitative data: the commonly discussed method of analytic induction (Znaniecki, 1968), and the less well known logical analysis (Williams, 1981a; 1981b; 1990) and will discuss their particular application to focus group data. The section will illustrate a number of issues that arise in the use of such methods with this type of data.

Analytic induction or deviant case analysis   Probably the most commonly used method of systematically testing hypotheses in qualitative analysis is that of analytic induction, which is described in many methods texts (Bulmer, 1984; Hammersley, 1989; Hammersley and Atkinson, 1995; Seale, 1999; Silverman, 1993), and is illustrated by a few empirical examples. It is necessary to describe the method generally before discussing its application to focus group data.

Analytic induction was developed by Znaniecki (1968) as an alternative to the statistical method in developing causal laws or generalizations. Robinson summarizes the claims made by Znaniecki about analytic induction:

> He holds that analytic induction gives us universal statements, of the form 'All S are P', instead of mere correlations to which there are always exceptions. He holds that analytic induction gives us exhaustive knowledge of the situation under study, so that further study will not and cannot reveal anything new. Finally, he holds that analytic induction leads us to genuinely causal laws. (Robinson, 1951: 812)

Analytic induction, then, is a means to derive explanatory hypotheses which apply to all the data available on a particular phenomena or problem (Frankland and Bloor, 1999), the crux of the method being the use of negative evidence to force revision of those hypotheses. The process is multi-stage and can be described as a series of steps to be followed (Hammersley, 1989; Hammersley and Atkinson, 1995; Seale, 1999). The researcher begins by defining the phenomenon or problem to be explained. She/he then views data from one case and derives an initial hypothesis which attempts to explain that phenomenon or problem. One-by-one, cases are compared to this hypothesis, to see whether they confirm or refute it. If a 'deviant case' (one where the data from the particular case does not fit the hypothesis) is found, this is taken to show that the hypothesis does not yet fit the available evidence (Sutherland and Cressey, 1960) and one of two courses are taken. First, the hypothesis can be refined so that it comes to embrace the refuting evidence:

> This definition must be more precise than the first one, and it may not be formulated *solely* to exclude a negative case. The negative case is viewed as a sign that something is wrong with the hypothesis, and redefinition takes place so that the cases of behavior being explained will be homogeneous. (Sutherland and Cressey, 1960: 68)

This may result in a relatively minor revision of the hypothesis, such as adding a further clause to it (Frankland and Bloor, 1999), or may lead to more significant revision of the hypothesis, as shown in the examples that follow. Alternative to this, the original definition of the phenomena or problem is revised in a manner that limits the population to which it is applicable, thus making the case which contains the negative evidence irrelevant to the analysis. For example, a hypothesis concerning the key stresses faced by working mothers may be found to apply only to those who work full time and not part time, or a hypothesis concerning the consumption of alcohol applying only to men and not women. This process, of comparing hypothesis with data and revising either the original proposition or the hypothesis, is repeated with more cases until no further negative evidence is found. By way of a check on this final hypothesis, cases which do not contain the defined behaviour may be studied, to make sure that the conditions of the hypothesis are *not* present (Sutherland and Cressey, 1960: 68–69).

The analytic induction method is progressive, each revision of the hypothesis building on the previous hypothesis (Lindesmith, 1947) and is basically comparative (Hammersley and Atkinson, 1995; Silverman, 1993), comparing the hypothesis with the available evidence. Note also that the phenomenon to be explained and the explanatory hypothesis are achieved, as far as possible, inductively.

The process of hypothesis development illustrates the potential importance in the analysis of having socio-demographic details of participants. These can be collected at the beginning of the focus group session, or may be available from related research in which group members have participated (see Chapter 3, section on pre-group self-completion questionnaires). Thought should be given at piloting to the sorts of details that might be required for the analysis. This may be basic details such as age and gender, or may include more detailed information related to the purpose of the research, such as smoking behaviour, work status, or other aspects of health.

Znaniecki's methods are best illustrated using empirical examples. The most commonly quoted of these are Lindesmith's (1947) study of opiate use and Cressey's (1953) study of embezzlement. In addition, the method has been used by Bloor (1978) in a study of ENT (ear, nose and throat) specialists, and with focus group data in a study of adolescent smoking behaviour (Frankland and Bloor, 1999). Two of these examples will be used for illustration here.

Lindesmith's (1947) study of opiate addiction centred on the fact that some people who use opiates become addicted while others do not. Lindesmith formulated an initial hypothesis, that those who know what drug they are taking and experience withdrawal on stopping become addicted while those who are not aware do not become addicted. He describes how a case was soon found which negated the former part of the hypothesis. A second hypothesis was formulated, being that it is those who recognize withdrawal who become addicted and without this recognition addiction does not occur. Again, cases to refute this were found and a third hypothesis was necessary; that those who become addicted recognize their withdrawal and seek further use of the drug with the express purpose of relieving their distress. Lindesmith states that no evidence was found to refute this final hypothesis.

Using data from focus groups, the group, not the individual, is used as the case for analysis purposes. In a study of adolescent smoking behaviour, Frankland and Bloor (1999) used the analytic induction method to attempt to explain the concept of peer pressure on giving up smoking. In this case analysis involved the successive development of three hypotheses. The first hypothesis stated that adolescents who are thinking of quitting smoking fear the threat of peer pressure in the form of bullying and exclusion from their friendship group, and that they expect active encouragement to continue smoking and a passive pressure from seeing others smoking. On consideration of the next case, a reformulation of the hypothesis was required, as pressure was shown to be related to the number of quitters: pressure to continue smoking was perceived as strongest for a lone quitter, but where more than one person is attempting to give up smoking, these people have greater pooled resources to counteract the pressure. A third revision was required since participants described how their peer group would not exclude a person who quit smoking. The final hypothesis, therefore made a distinction between 'real friends' (who would not exclude) and people who 'use you for fags' (who would). At this point in the analysis it became clear that there were insufficient data to develop this distinction between type of friends further, and the analysis was forced to close. There is further discussion of this issue of premature closure below.

The method of analytic induction is not without criticism (see, for example, Robinson, 1951; Hammersley and Atkinson 1995) and there are theoretical debates over whether the method actually achieves what Znaniecki claimed (Robinson, 1951). In its use with focus groups, analytic induction has been shown to meet with a number of problems (Frankland and Bloor, 1999). The method is however of interest for analysis of this type of data, as it systematizes the analysis process by providing a number of clear steps for the researcher to follow. This can be particularly useful in helping to see a clear path when faced with hundreds of pages of seemingly chaotic focus group transcripts. By insisting that the researcher should search for evidence to refute his or her hypothesis, the method also helps prevent closure of the analysis before the explanation is complete (Robinson, 1951) and prevents selective use of evidence to support a hypothesis.

The issue of premature closure of analysis hinted at above is one of the problems with applying analytic induction to focus group data (and to other forms of qualitative data, see Bloor, 1978). In the example of the adolescent smoking project (Frankland and Bloor, 1999) it was not possible to develop the distinction between friends who 'use you for fags' and 'real friends' beyond the existence of the concept, as this had not been dealt with in sufficient depth in the focus groups (not naturally by the group nor picked up by the moderator). The problem clearly results from not realizing while conducting the focus groups that a particular theme would be an important theme for the analysis, and thus not following up the theme in the group to provide sufficient depth of data for analysis. This begs the question of how does the researcher know that they have sufficient data and can end data collection. This is not only a question of how many groups to run (see Chapter 2) but also one of having sufficient depth of data on the important issues. As Bloor reports in his study of ENT specialists, case study research, through which analytic induction was developed, allows the researcher to periodically leave the field to develop hypotheses, and then return to the field to follow those up with further data collection (Bloor, 1978). In focus group research, it is rarely possible, for practical reasons, to reform a group in order to follow up a hypothesis (although it may be possible to form a new group to act as proxy for the group). In the study by Frankland and Bloor (1999) the focus groups had taken place within school time and the number of groups had previously been agreed with the school, plus by the time the analysis had reached this stage, pupils had moved to a new school year. It was thus not practical to ask to reconvene the groups. In such circumstances, the researcher must decide where data collection should end before having carried out detailed analysis (Frankland and Bloor, 1999). In order to avoid such problems without resorting to collecting far more data (and running far more groups) than is necessary (making the analysis appear even more overwhelming) the researcher should try to focus through piloting and early analysis on those themes which are likely to be important for the final analysis. These can then be followed in sufficient depth in the groups.

The second difficulty in applying analytic induction to focus group data relates more directly to the nature of the data. As previously stated, transcripts often contain speech which is unfinished, as participants are interrupted, or the conversation goes off in a different direction. Some of these uncertainties can be cleared up at the indexing stage, as described above. The analyst will still need to interpret these divergences when looking for deviant cases: it may be unclear whether such unfinished extracts are in opposition to the hypothesis and so warrant its revision. (This illustrates the important role of the moderator in clearing up ambiguities and in asking people to complete what they were saying, although with the best of moderation, ambiguities are still likely to occur.) It is important, if ambiguity cannot be resolved, that the analyst is prepared to exclude the case from the analysis (Frankland and Bloor, 1999), rather than to amend the hypothesis on the grounds of uncertainty.

Logical analysis   Less well known than analytic induction as a method of systematic analysis is that of logical analysis. The method has been developed and discussed by Williams (1981a; 1981b; 1990) in relation to a study of old age and chronic illness. Williams deems the method suitable for analysis of certain topics, 'in particular for revealing the interrelation of definitions, beliefs or evaluations, whether individual or cultural' (Williams, 1981b: 182). Williams states the aim of logical analysis as: 'simply to reveal the logical shape of an informant's ideas. Instead of measuring the informant against the researcher's logic, the research attempts to elicit the informant's logic' (Williams, 1981a: 141).

While there are no examples of the method being applied to focus group data, logical analysis can be seen to lend itself to this purpose. Like analytic induction, the process of logical analysis can be described as a series of steps. First, the analyst searches for premises within the data, that are of the type 'If A, then B' (such as 'If I do not keep up my normal activity, I make my condition worse' (Williams, 1990: 337)). Second, these premises are grouped and represented with a typical premise for that group. Third, the analyst explores connections between one group of premises and another (Williams, 1990). In discussing the use of the method, Williams highlights the problem of dealing with data where the person holds two contradictory sets of premises (Williams, 1981b), something he states to be quite common. This illustrates that the use of logical analysis with focus groups would result in similar problems to analytic induction – how to interpret the uncertainty within the data that sometimes occurs in focus groups.

Thus, the interactive nature of focus groups, which leads to some uncertainty in the data, resulting from contradiction and unfinished speech, causes problems for systematic approaches to analysis. The possible solutions to this have been discussed already: data collection should be carefully focused following piloting and initial analysis; moderators should work hard to eliminate any contradiction or inter-rupted speech; and the analyst should be prepared to remove from analysis cases where ambiguity cannot be resolved. This will not eliminate the problem entirely but will help to minimize its impact on the use of the method (Frankland and Bloor, 1999).

Feedback groups

It has already been suggested (see Chapter 1) that focus groups can be held at the end of a study with the purpose of allowing participants to comment on preliminary analysis. A draft report or synopsis forms the focusing exercise, and participants are asked for their views. Comments are then used to extend and deepen, although not to validate the analysis. Focus groups may be the best method by which to carry out such an exercise, in that they minimize interviewer bias (Bloor, 1997).

In a study of therapeutic communities, Bloor et al. (1988) ran a series of focus groups with staff and ex-patients in order to collect participants' responses to draft research reports. Bloor (1997) describes how reactions to reports may be supportive or dismissive, but how, in the latter case, discussion can lead to greater understanding on the part of the researcher, which in turn can lead to a deepening of the analysis. Such an exercise is not necessarily unproblematic, and Bloor (1997) reports a number of misgivings he had with the process. First, participants are generally unversed in carrying out such critical appraisal and may not study reports in adequate depth, or may be too close to the subject for judgement to be made. Bloor (1978) suggests that requirements to carry out the process are thus an adequate (but not too high) level of commitment to the research, to promote a useful degree of criticism. Second, participants' comments are context specific and are subject to change over time. Emerson and Pollner (1988, quoted in Bloor, 1997) report how members of mobile Psychiatric Emergency Teams were unwilling to agree with any criticisms of their service for fear that these would lead to enforcement of threatened cutbacks. Third, participants may agree with the analysis for reasons which differ to the thinking of the researcher, taking, for example, a minor topic and making it the central issue.

The execution of focus groups based on a preliminary analysis can thus extend and deepen the analysis, but as a method (like any method) is not problem free. As with the original analysis, the researcher has to interpret these participants' comments on the analysis (Bloor, 1997). There are also practical issues in carrying out such an exercise. The focusing exercise may be a pre-circulated synopsis, or the group may begin with a brief run through of the results. The former method will only be successful if all group members come to the group having read the report, but the latter has the disadvantage of allowing little time to reflect on the results before comment. Chapter 2 has already discussed the problems with reconvening groups, and it may be that if comment on the analysis is what is required a newly formed and similarly composed group will need to be used as a proxy.

Where it is possible to reconvene a group, as is more likely where focus groups utilize pre-existing groups, the exercise of feeding back results can have other benefits, in terms, for example, of helping gain access and as a courtesy to group members (Bloor, 1997).

Reporting of speech

In writing up an analysis of focus group data, the researcher needs to keep in mind two issues pertinent to the reporting of speech. First, it has been suggested that the way speech is reported, in terms of punctuation, spelling, editing out of faltering and the like, affects the 'readability' of the text and also the way in which the reported speaker is perceived by the reader (Atkinson, 1992). As Atkinson states:

> If we quote a completely unvarnished version . . . then it may be so difficult to read (because so fragmentary, so far from standard discourse, so full of hesitations and similar phenomena) that the sense of the utterances is all but lost to view. (1992: 25–26)

It is at the reporting stage that any editing of text and of transcription conventions takes place, in order to render it readable. Second, it has been suggested that with focus groups, longer quotations should be given, in order to provide some of the context to the speech. Myers and Macnaghten (1999) argue that, as a minimum, the preceding turn of speech should be reported for this end.

Conclusion

Focus group data are distinct from other forms of qualitative data, and their interactive nature needs to be taken into account at all stages of analysis. A full and thorough audiotranscription is necessary within academic research. This needs to include all speakers and all speech, even that which is unfinished or interrupted. Speakers should be identified where possible, and notation used to indicate aspects of speech such as interruption. Once transcribed, data are indexed to bring under one heading all data relating to a particular theme. The analyst needs to keep in view the context of any extract of speech and to follow the arguments of individuals and the group through the transcript. Indexed data can be stored and retrieved either manually or by using one of the qualitative data computer programs. In order that rigorous analysis takes place, a method which lays down step-by-step procedures, such as analytic induction or logical analysis can be used. It is desirable to use a systematic approach such as these, but in applying them to focus group data specific issues pertaining to the nature of the data need to be noted and addressed. Feedback groups may be used to extend and deepen the analysis and may have practical advantages such as easing access and as a courtesy to participants. In reporting focus group data, the researcher needs to think about the readability of any data presented and about the degree of context the reader will need in order to make sense of the data.

EXERCISES

1 What are the benefits of a method of analysis such as analytic induction or logical analysis; what are the problems with use of these analytic methods with focus group data; why do these arise; are there any solutions?

2 What purpose can feedback groups have in focus group research; what issues need to be kept in mind when carrying out such an exercise?

3 Why is context a particularly important issue within the analysis of focus group data; how should the analyst account for this?

5

Virtual focus groups

CONTENTS

Increasingly, the social sciences are harnessing various forms of computer-mediated communications to collect both quantitative and qualitative research data. In many ways this development has echoed that of the use of the telephone as a data collection tool early in the twentieth century. The telephone offers speedy access to geographically wide-spread groups for minimal cost. The participant enjoys a degree of anonymity that may encourage more open and honest answers, free from the influences of the presence or appearance of the interviewer. However, early uses of telephone surveys were hindered by a clear social bias that resulted from the unequal ownership of the facility (Babbie, 1992). While most traditional, 'terrestrial' data collection methods have developed telephone-based equivalents, and latterly computer-mediated equivalents, the 'technologization' of the focus group has bypassed the essentially one-to-one medium of the telephone, and may therefore have seemed an inherently terrestrial method. However, in recent years, 'virtual focus groups' have combined the principles of the generation of data through group interaction with the communications technologies that have emerged.

By 1997 there were 47 million Internet users world-wide, with a further 38 million intending to get online in the following year. Projections estimate that by 2002 there will be 175 million users world-wide (Branestorm, 1998). While user demographics have traditionally been marked, the introduction of free Internet Service Providers (ISPs) in the UK, such as Freeserve, Netscape Online and Tescos, will not only result in an even greater than predicted growth in user numbers, but also make Internet access a more realistic option for lower income groups.

The recent growth of computer-mediated communication heralded by this growth in Internet subscription has created an alternative, common-place convention for group interaction. Both one-to-one and one-to-many communications on a range of subjects and issues as diverse as human experience have flourished, and such interaction can be harnessed or administered for research purposes in a focus group style. Virtual focus groups are not the 'future of focus group research': they can not and should not be thought of as a replacement for the focus group in its traditional form. However virtual focus groups do offer a useful stable-mate in the focus group tradition, and a worthwhile new tool for the social researcher.

Recent uses of virtual focus groups in the social sciences

Although 'virtual focus group' is both a familiar term and method in market research, its use in academic research has so far been limited. The administration of questionnaires via computerized communications has been a far more popular development (see Witmer et al., 1999). However, many that have embraced this innovation are unaware that there is a suspicion of online survey research among many online participants because of its quantitative nature (Kendall, 1999), and thus a reluctance to participate in such studies by many users. At the other end of the spectrum, covert observation and collection of naturally occurring online discussions and communities has been a common approach among researchers of cyberphenomena. While bearing some similarities to the virtual focus groups discussed here, such research falls outside of the definition of virtual focus group in exactly the same way that a covertly observed real life discussion does not constitute a real life focus group. Such 'harvesting' (the term for the collection of material from computer-mediated interactions without prior consent) is viable and legal, and may be attractive as a speedy way of collecting rich data (Sharf, 1999). However, it poses ethical problems, because like online surveys it flouts the conventions of the medium's users. Harvesting online conversations also limits the amount of background information the researcher is privy to prior to investing their time and resources in collecting the data. Given the flaws in these two extremes of online research method that have courted popularity, the slow development of virtual focus groups has been a surprising missed opportunity.

One of the first documented uses of virtual focus groups in academic social research was Murray's (1997) study of health professionals with an expertise in computer-mediated communication. The combination of geographic dispersal and familiarity with computerized communications made the use of a virtual focus group singularly appropriate in the research. Like traditional focus groups, Murray's virtual groups consisted of 6 to 8 members, although it was acknowledged that larger groups might be appropriate to achieve the level and style of discussion sought by the researcher. In Murray's smaller groups, simultaneous conversational threads did not develop. 'Threading' is characteristic of naturally occurring online discussions, and refers to the simultaneous conduct of multiple topics of conversation. To an observer, threading may make the discussion appear chaotic, but participants are usually adept at maintaining distinctions between the different threads of a discussion. Using an asynchronous discussion form (mailing list) precluded the mirroring of the length of discussion from traditional focus groups. Murray's groups ran for approximately 4 weeks, which allowed time for the discussion to develop, but encouraged active discussion by signalling the finite nature of the list. Murray found that too high a level of questioning from the researcher resulted in contributions constituting of serial direct answering by the participants to the researcher, rather than stimulating discussion among the participants.

Robson's use of virtual focus groups was part of a project on employment experiences of inflammatory bowel disease sufferers. Having conducted face-to-face research with members of a 'real life' patient support group, participants in online patient support networks were recruited for a virtual focus group. Like Murray, a closed subscription private distribution list was used, but larger numbers were recruited, with 57 participants subscribed. The larger group size allowed the threading of discussions, with multiple topics simultaneously discussed, while the group nonetheless remained open, responsive and familiar with each other. The discussion ran for 2 months, with minimal guidance or questioning from the researcher, beyond defining the general area of discussion and providing opening questions at the outset.

Unlike Murray's and Robson's focus groups, Stewart et al. (1998) conducted a synchronous online focus group discussion. Their pilot study of young women's health risk perceptions was conducted primarily to investigate the usefulness of the Internet as a qualitative public health research tool. Participants were located in four sites in China and Australia, with the chat software configured for private access by them only. The discussions took place in a parent conference area which had four sub-conference areas, with one online facilitator who entered and exited the different chat rooms during the discussions. The primary role of the facilitator was to ensure that all the discussion topics were covered, and they made minimal contributions to the discussions. The discussions lasted for nearly twice the expected one hour duration, and were described by the researchers as serious and entertaining exchanges. Facilitating the discussions was described as being more problematic than is usually the case in traditional focus groups, or as would be the case in other asynchronous forms of virtual focus group, because of the speed and frequency with which topics changed. Thus, it was harder to ensure that all the planned topics for discussion were covered by participants, and also harder to probe issues. However, Stewart et al. (1998) concluded that the study demonstrated a viable methodological approach in cross-cultural research, highlighting a similarity in public discourse about health risk issues in a way that traditional face-to-face forms of research could not.

Administering virtual focus groups

Computer-mediated discussion forms are continually developing, and the social dynamics of discussions vary between these different types of online forum. Features such as whether the discussion is synchronous or asynchronous and how easily non-participants can view discussions impact the kind of discussion that results (Kendall, 1999). Deciding which medium to use is therefore an important consideration when embarking on a virtual focus group project.

Computer-mediated discussion

The first 'virtual communities' of communication technology were Bulletin Board Services, which developed over 20 years ago and are described by Stone (1995) as public letter writing perceived as conversations. Initially these were limited mainly to electronics experimenters, computer builders and ham radio buffs (i.e. mainly white males). These disparate systems developed into a 'tree' organization, giving coherence and continuity to the emerging 'community'. The interactions that Bulletin Board Services and their successors (such as Role-Playing Games, Multiple User Domains, Newsgroups and Distribution Lists) now host relate to a wide variety of human activities (Langford, 1995a). They are, according to Stone (1995) social acts that allow participants unrivalled means of experimenting with new perspectives and identities. 'Habitat' is a more recent Multiple User Domain, incorporating graphics instead of text to create environments. Here, the ratio of men to women 'signing up' is 4 to 1, but given the freedom to create themselves as a character in the domain, the ratio of male to female characters is 3 to 1. This discrepancy reflects not only an indication of the potential for users to experiment with their own gender identities, but also an acknowledgement that, because of the predominance of male users in the environment, a 'female' presence will attract attention and give the user greater prominence in the activities of the domain (Stone, 1995). So, although this is ostensibly a 'non-physical' environment, users can control the effects of physicality in social situations to achieve desired ends.

Although often seen as being a less accurate reflection of the thoughts than verbal data, the 'mute evidence' of written data can offer physical endurance and the (sometimes necessary) convenience of both spatial and temporal distance between subject and researcher (Hodder, 1994). It may be felt that written material exchanged by cable to an anonymous world-wide audience may lack the richness of other forms of communication and interaction. Stone (1995) argues that technology *can* convey more than 'just' words: sensations of sight, smell, taste, touch and hearing can all be compressed into audible codes and exchanged through single mode, narrow bandwidth communication. Like the interactions of the phone sex industry described by Young (1994), sensory experiences are translated into verbal (and therefore transcribable) form and transmitted down telephone lines, where they are reconstituted by the recipient. The interactions in 'cyberspace' are, Stone asserts, social in character and do have meaning as such.

Media such as Bulletin Board Services, newsgroups and distribution lists can be perceived as group conversations of open letters, given an immediacy that terrestrial written communication can never offer. Although users often perceive e-mails as transitory and impermanent (and so write in a style reflecting this), once sent, an e-mail can be stored and disseminated in ways over which the author has no control (Langford, 1995a).

This combination of immediacy and collapsed spatial distance that Internet and computer-mediated communication offers allows the development of virtual communities of individuals that may be both geographically highly dispersed and physically immobile. Sveilich (1995) argues that the feelings of isolation and confusion that an inflammatory bowel disease sufferer experiences upon diagnosis can be compounded by a lack of physical energy, which may in turn inhibit participation in a 'traditional' patient support group. Her response to her own diagnosis was to start posting messages on IBM's Prodigy Bulletin Board Service, establishing the first medical bulletin board on Prodigy. As there were no other patient support groups on Prodigy's Bulletin Board Service at that time, initial messages were posted under the 'Food' section. Soon though, a thriving 'Medical' section of the Bulletin Board Service evolved, as sufferers of inflammatory bowel disease and other conditions began to communicate with fellow sufferers.

Does the creation of such communication groups for research purposes amount to a form of focus group? Characteristically, a focus group is a discussion around a given topic between 6 to 12 participants, which is monitored, guided if necessary and recorded by the researcher. The distinguishing feature of focus groups is the explicit use of group interaction to produce data. The more familiar, comfortable and unthreatening the setting of the focus group, the more open the discussion can be expected to be (Kitzinger, 1994a; Morgan, 1988). Therefore, if we accept that the interactions of cyberspace are social, the most accurate or 'naturalistic' recreation of these interactions for a focus group discussion would be using this medium.

'Traditional' focus group methodology has already harnessed technological advancements: the discussion of sensitive topics in focus groups can be helped by the use of teleconference calls allowing anonymity and more open responses (Smith, 1995; White and Thompson, 1995). High technology options such as electronic answer buttons, rheostats, computer keyboards and interactive videoconferencing have all been used to improve comfort and convenience for the client in market research focus groups (Krueger, 1995). It appears, then, only logical to extend this 'comfort and convenience' to participants: for 'Internet communities' this amounts to nothing more than the creation of an appropriate setting for the discussion to take place in. As the use of computer-mediated communications has become more commonplace, discussions using the medium no longer need to be 'about' the technology, or groups arising from the technology, offering instead simply another means by which groups of individuals can interact. Ominously, research in marketing and manufacturing market analysis had experimented with the use of computer-mediated communications, but its use in qualitative social research had not been described until the late 1990s (Murray, 1997).

Clearly, despite the rapid expansion of the Internet, its use as a research tool will reflect the demographically based biases of current usage patterns of the medium, and uses of the Internet for research purposes has as a result been very limited. Although the biases that Internet usage currently contain must not be overlooked, they are declining and will continue to do so. Therefore, the Internet should be recognized as an appropriate social research tool whose potential goes well beyond literature searches and statistical sources.

Setting up discussions for research purposes

There are a number of different kinds of e-mail and Internet based discussion forums, each with its own strengths and weaknesses as a potential research tool. Creating an online discussion forum to collect data involves a number of requirements and restrictions which define which type of discussion channel is appropriate.

The earliest forms of online discussion took the form of Bulletin Board Services. These are telephone (rather than Internet) dial-up services which do not require an account with an Internet service provider, and as such have been available to a broader range of computer users. Although personal, home use is rapidly expanding, Internet access is still heavily dominated by users from the academic community and commercial organizations. However, because Bulletin Board Services are not connected to the Internet, users of telephone dial-up systems tend to be far more geographically concentrated than other discussion forums, due to the telephone call costs involved in accessing them.

'Internet Relay Chat' (IRC) is real time discussion between users, and can be accessed via both Bulletin Board Services, and Internet software.

While this does give the most immediate form of online interaction, and dialogue most akin to 'real life' conversation, global discussion is hindered by the different time zones that users are in. While one-to-one IRC conversations can be scheduled with relative ease, group discussions on a global basis at a time convenient to all are virtually impossible to organize. Other, asynchronous, forms of group interaction offer similar levels of intimacy and familiarity, but avoid the temporal inconveniences that IRC, like 'real life' interactions, is subject to. Administering a discussion through IRC is relatively straightforward. Any user can create a channel on an IRC network, control who enters the discussion and even remove disruptive participants. However, it is not possible to disguise information identifying the Internet connection (and therefore possibly also the identity) of any user on an IRC network from other participants.

Newsgroups are Internet based discussions which can be accessed with the necessary Internet software, or with some e-mail programs. Visually, newsgroups are very user-friendly: messages are organized according to topic into conversation 'threads' that participants can directly follow and reply to. However, access to a newsgroup can not be restricted by its participants, and as e-mail messages contain 'headers' identifying the sender which are difficult to remove, contributions can not be anonymized. Any research quoting or explicitly referring to a posted article would be unable to prevent the identification of subjects by other users. In practical terms, newsgroups are much harder to set up, requiring a poll to demonstrate the demand for a proposed new newsgroup. Although existing newsgroup discussions can and have been recorded for research purposes, the observation of naturally occurring interactions falls outside of the definition of a virtual focus group as the discussion is not created for the purposes of the research.

Distribution lists are e-mail based and have a single central e-mail address to which all contributions are sent. Messages sent to this address are automatically forwarded to all the subscribers to the list. Distribution list programs offer a number of options that can give the protection that newsgroups lack. Once selected, the list of participants can be 'closed', preventing anyone else from subscribing to the list. Information about the list can be defined as 'private', preventing the access of information about who the subscribers are and what the topic of discussion is by non-subscribers. Distribution lists can also be 'moderated', allowing the articulation of a role akin to that of a traditional focus group moderator. In moderated lists individual messages are not immediately distributed to all subscribers, but are sent to the moderator, who can also gather individual messages to compile a single composite posting (a 'digest') that is distributed to the subscribers periodically (for example, either when a certain number of messages have been received, or on a given day of the week). Thus, moderation reduces and regulates the flow of messages that subscribers receive, allowing subjects to exercise a greater degree of discretion in participation. Moderation also allows messages from subscribers to be organized according to topic (as in a newsgroup), and the opportunity for the researcher to guide the discussion in the way a focus group moderator might. A moderated distribution list can attempt to seek progressively more agreement, so acting something like an electronic Delphi Group. The Delphi technique seeks to aggregate and distil the opinion of experts by summarizing and synthesizing contributions or opinions, by seeking written responses rather than face-to-face verbal contributions (Adler and Ziglio, 1996).

The different kinds of online discussion forum used for a virtual focus group raise different issues about the conduct of the focus group. Asynchronous discussions are much easier for the researcher to actively moderate, as the asynchronicity offers time to consider and compose interventions. Robson's distribution list participants who had reservations or queries about aspects of their contributions contacted the researcher privately for clarification before submitting a message to the group. One high profile participant in the research had specific concerns about being identified through her contributions, and double checked issues about the anonymity and confidentiality of her posts before her initial contribution. In asynchronous discussions, moderators have greater opportunity to encourage participation from those who read but do not contribute to the discussion ('lurkers'), without being distracted from an ongoing real time discussion, and without highlighting the participants reticence 'in front of' the rest of the group. Synchronous discussion groups tend to be far more dynamic and chaotic, limiting the amount of intervention or control the moderator has in the discussion, as well as strictly limiting the amount of pre-submission deliberation on the part of contributors. Thus, synchronous discussions are harder for the moderator to nurture or adjust once the discussion is underway, and require much greater familiarity with and skill in online discussion on the part of the researcher.

Strengths and weaknesses of virtual focus groups

The low costs involved in running virtual focus groups make them a particularly attractive way of including research participants who might otherwise be beyond the reach of a project. Expenditure on recording equipment, room hire, travel costs, refreshment costs and audio transcription costs incurred in face-to-face focus groups are replaced by the minimal costs of the electronic storage of data gathered using what is now standard specification computer hardware. The costs associated with the amount of time researchers can spend conducting focus group fieldwork are also reduced significantly by the absence of the need to travel. In turn this means that virtual focus groups need not be time-limited in the same way as face-to-face focus groups, allowing much more extensive discussions to develop.

Inevitably there is a clear difference between the data generated by a virtual focus group and the transcripts that any traditional focus group discussion would produce. Virtual focus group transcripts will not follow the transcription conventions described in Chapter 4, as the text should be analysed in the way it was formatted and arranged by the contributor in the original discussion. Use of characters, capitals, hard returns and even colour have meaning in the argot of computer-mediated communications, and should be preserved. Contributions to virtual focus groups represent, formed, considered and well-articulated responses and contributions, often dealing with issues raised by several different messages at once. Several discussion 'threads' can be simultaneously active at any one time, with participants following and responding to these. Unlike a face-to-face discussion, contributors are not subject to interruption or distraction, and can revise their contributions prior to submission to the rest of the group. This refinement can take place without any delay or intrusion in the process of receiving ('hearing') the contributions to the discussion.

As with a traditional focus group discussion, virtual focus groups generate data from the interaction of the participants. Groups can be much larger in size than a traditional focus group, as greater group size does not interfere with an individual's ability or willingness to contribute: the contributions of the meekest, the most ponderous and the most controversial are sent and received as equals. Murray's (1997) virtual focus groups, like traditional focus groups, numbered 6–8 participants, although larger groups may sometimes be needed to promote the levels of discussion and interaction sought, and to facilitate the 'threading' of discussions, which did not occur in his smaller groups. Robson's virtual focus group included over 50 participants (a relatively modest number for a distribution list), which did facilitate the threading of discussions, but which did not stifle a lively and responsive discussion.

The use of a distribution list as a data collection tool can undoubtedly be valuable, but would not be appropriate to all research settings. A number of factors made their employment in Robson's project appropriate, and these criteria can be used to gauge the appropriateness of the method in other studies:

1   There was an existing, well-established and active computer-mediated support community for the target population of the research.
2   The subject area of the research made it less unusual for the population to have access to and knowledge of e-mail communication.
3   The intended topic of discussion comfortably crossed national boundaries.

Clearly, despite the rapid expansion of e-mail and the Internet, its use as a research tool will reflect the demographically based biases of current usage patterns of the medium, in much the same way as early telephone surveys were hindered by the clear social biases that resulted from the unequal ownership of that facility (Babbie, 1992). Thus, at present, as Schmidt (1997) suggests, electronic methodologies can only be considered a valuable alternative to traditional techniques for research which targets specific and narrowly defined populations with easy access to the Internet and e-mail, and its use should always be offset against the wider considerations of population access to the medium and the limitations of the plentiful data that are generated (Selwyn and Robson, 1998). The main caution that remains with this research approach regards the biases within the sample. Nonetheless, e-mail and Internet communications should be recognized as an appropriate social research tool whose potential transcends its current restricted use. As Coomber contends, the demographic disparities that currently restrict online research are fast diminishing: 'the relative exclusivity of current Internet use needs to be considered seriously but does not preclude attempts to do useful and informative sociological research' (Coomber, 1997: para 1.1).

Recreating the essential elements of a focus group discussion in a written online environment can be achieved with great success, generating valuable, rich data, and clearly establishing the viability of such an approach.

BOX 5.1 SUMMARY OF THE STRENGTHS AND WEAKNESSES OF VIRTUAL FOCUS GROUPS

Strengths	Weaknesses
Fast, low cost.	Requires a level of technical competence, and familiarity with the discussion medium used.
Offers convenience to the researcher and participants.	
Offers access to dispersed, immobile, or difficult to convene populations.	Inherits population biases of Internet users.
Encourages revelation on sensitive topics.	Difficult to detect deceit or probe issues.
Reduces interviewer effect.	Rapport can be difficult to establish.
Data is ready transcribed with no room for transcriber error.	Data lack non-verbal cues and information.
Appropriate to the conventions of naturally occurring computer-mediated interaction.	

Ethical considerations of online research

The already highly fragmented character of the Internet has blocked the development of a global ethical policy policing its use, and the acceptable limits of its use for academic research purposes (Langford, 1995a; 1995b; Robson and Robson, 1999). Only by the use of the medium, with heed to conventional ethical and methodological criteria as well as the emerging field of Internet ethics, will answers to these issues develop. Ethical considerations in online research must take account of both the codes of conduct that relate to behaviour in computer-mediated groups and communities, and codes of conduct relating to the practice of social research.

How we use the Internet and what is deemed as acceptable behaviour is governed through an amalgam of service providers acceptable use policies, codes of conduct and the implications of certain laws.

Internet service providers acceptable use policies and terms of use are probably the most structured control of how we use the Internet specifically. They give the service provider some control over the way you use the Internet when accessing it via their network, and generally have a strong emphasis on responsible use of the network and not doing anything that would have an effect on the availability of the network to others. Informal codes of conduct ('netiquette') were developed naturally by the online community as the Internet grew and developed. They outline standard practices for the various services available over the Internet (e-mail, newsgroups, IRC, etc.) and define how to behave and what is unacceptable behaviour within these areas. Within these guidelines there is a strong emphasis on observing the guidelines and culture of the group or medium you are participating in. Legal issues relating to the use of computerized communications are complex, and a comprehensive review of these is beyond the scope of this chapter. There are a variety of laws internationally that relate to the use of computers and communication technology. In Britain, the Data Protection Act 1998 and the Computer Misuse Act 1990 are of particular relevance, relating to an individual's right to privacy and knowledge that any personal information that they give to companies or organizations about themselves is protected to some degree by the law. Although attention to legal issues pertaining to computerized communications is important, in general terms, adherence to Acceptable Use Polices (AUPs) and netiquette will usually meet with legal requirements. Covering all of the areas outlined above, organizations like the Internet Society, Computer Professional for Social Responsibility (CPSR) and the Electronic Frontier Foundation, along with many others, work on behalf of the online community to maintain the Internet as a free open global community available and beneficial to all. They are involved in the continuous evolution and development of online codes of conduct and with the development of any regulations or laws that have a direct impact on the use of the

Internet. They are also highly involved in the use of the Internet and it implications on an individuals civil rights or what has become known as cyber rights. For example, the CPSR have produced a set of electronic privacy guidelines, which states that:

> The ethical responsibility for privacy protection lies with those who would violate that privacy, and with those who design and provide the systems where the violations can occur.
> (http://www.cpsr.org/program/privacy/privacy8.htm)

The central issues of professional and ethical codes of conduct that have been developed for social research generally relate to issues of informed consent, of privacy, confidentiality and dignity, of the avoidance of harm. Seeking consent from those who are recruited as part of a 'virtual focus group' set up for research purposes is relatively straightforward and comparable to eliciting consent in more traditional situations. Ostensibly the idea that identifying information should be kept confidential for the purposes of any written report of the research seems fairly straightforward. However, the risk of deductive disclosure is very real in research in computerized communities. Complete anonymity is, of course, almost impossible to guarantee, as information about the origin of a computer transmitted message is for most users, almost impossible to remove. The absence of anonymity in research does not of course mean researchers cannot guarantee confidentiality to research subjects. However, in computer-mediated research this is more difficult to do. Traditional procedures for storage of data and anonymizing participants are complicated in a medium where a *record of the original data* is routinely available to others who have participated in the research – members of a virtual focus group all receive a copy of all of the postings. Any research quoting or explicitly referring to an article posted in any kind of group discussion cannot prevent the identification of the author of that message by others. In a traditional, terrestrial focus group, in order for any one participant to retain a copy of the original data requires conscious decision and great effort to secure that. In the computer-mediated research setting, conscious decision is required to *not* have such a record. As such, the American Sociological Association's (1997) statement of ethical practice that holds that researchers should: 'prevent data being published or released in a form which would permit the actual or potential identification of research participants' (http://www.asanet.org/ecoderev.htm) is virtually impossible to adhere to.

Much of this issue depends on definitions of computer-mediated communications being private or public forms of communication. Arguably, different kinds of online media differ in terms of their perceived degree of privacy that are afforded to them in their use. Privacy can occur within public situations (Elgesem, 1996, cited in Sharf, 1999), and crucially, because these communications are often perceived as private *by users*, greater intimacy and self-revelation are encouraged. To this end, only relevant data should be gathered, and it should be stored securely. Again, however diligently the researcher does this, they can have no ultimate control over material that will have been retained by any participants in the research, restricting the ability of the researcher to protect the researched from harm. Informing potential participants about the research to elicit consent to participate is not merely about explaining the research procedure, it must include information about the foreseeable uses to which the research findings will be put. But the ability to do this will inevitably be undermined in a setting where the research process and data can be so easily shared by others.

Conclusion

Emergent communications technologies have spawned new forms of group interaction which in turn now offer new ways of applying the principles of focus group research. Virtual focus groups offer speedy, convenient and low-cost options for gathering rich qualitative data from dispersed, immobile or difficult to convene populations. To succeed, use of the method needs to take account of any prevailing relevant population biases of Internet usership in relation to the research's target population, but beyond this restriction the opportunities are many and varied. Virtual focus groups can be seen as representing a response to the demand from developing computer-mediated communications to think about data collections in new and appropriate ways. As such, virtual focus groups are not a new method, but a new dimension of an established method, offering new opportunities in focus group research.

EXERCISE

Below are 2 extracts from online discussions about inflammatory bowel disease. How does the style of the two extracts differ? How do these extracts differ from a traditional face-to-face focus group?

Extract 1: Internet Relay Chat

<Susi2> i have a colonocopy [sic] comin up soon *yuk*
<Babyface> yuck, Susi2

* Babyface has had one BE (barium enema), two SBFTs (small bowel follow-thru), three colonoscopies, and an EGD (esophagogastroduodeno-scopy)

<Wings> Yeah, bm.
<Babyface> Of course, I met someone here once who had had 17 colono-
   scopies
<Babyface> I was shocked
<Susi2> one thing i will never have again is a barium enema. . no way. . no
   how. . EVER!
<Susi2> my doc wants me to have one a year
<Babyface> I second that, Susi2
<Babyface> Most emphatically
<Babyface> ewwwwwwwwww. . .t odenoscopy drugs
<Susi2> yeah. . they knock u out
<Babyface> pretty much
<Susi2> i never know a thing
<Babyface> I was shocked

*** Wings has quit IRC

<bagman> I never remembered my colonoscopys, the drugs always made mem
   forget
<Babyface> it was awful. . . that was the first test I'd ever had done. I tried to
   watch the screen but it was hard to concentrate after awhile
<Susi2> thats what diagnosed. . and i said then i would never do it again
<Babyface> Well, when I had my BE, I was misdiagnosed as having UC. I went
   into denial for two years before I got help again.
<Susi2> they put me to sleep with those. . . .
<bagman> Nothin like closed curcit TV, eh Baby ;)
<Babyface> Well, they put me to sleep with the first colonoscopy, but when I
   started groaning in pain, they had to stop the test.
<Babyface> hehehe bagman
<Susi2> bug. how old are u ?
<bagman> 35 here

Extract 2: Distribution list contribution

Hi everyone!

I failed to introduce myself in my first posting to the initial digest. My name
is Mark. I am 28 years old and live in Manitoba. I have had an ileostomy
for 13 years and I have not had any complications of any magnitude for
10 years. I feel very fortunate after reading some of the other people's
comments that I am able to live a relatively normal life. I guess I should
answer my own question about how do people plan their washroom
breaks at work. I am lucky that I can pretty much use the "facilities"
whenever I need to. I work as a computer database administrator and my
time is not based on any set lunch or washroom breaks.

As far as some of the other people comments, Paul wanted to know other peoples ideas about whether or not to hide their illness or be open about it. From my own perspective, I have no problem telling people if it happens to come up in conversation or if I feel it is an issue that should be explained such as being absent from work because of my disease. I have never consciously withheld the fact I wear an ileostomy in either my business or personal dealings.

That's it for now. I would like to say 'Hi' to fellow Canadian and ileostomate - Nicola.

Mark

6

Conclusions

CONTENTS

Various embarrassing social roles for sociologists have been proposed (or complacently claimed) in the past or the present: those of consultant 'social engineer' (see Carey's (1975) history of the Chicago School of sociology), or enlightened 'state counsellor' (Silverman's (1993) wry characterization of Bulmer's claim in his 1982 text *The Uses of Social Research*). Thankfully though, no-one has seriously proposed sociologists for the role of social prophet. So we are spared the professional necessity of making authoritative pronouncements on the future of focus groups in academic social research. But, just for the hell of it, we would prophesy that the current, faddish growth in popularity of focus group methods will not be maintained. Academic social research requires more of focus groups than just data on group reactions to toilet tissue campaigns, but these more complex requirements can only be met by expenditure of very high levels of researcher effort in group composition, recruitment, planning, conduct, transcription and analysis. Moreover, there are many topic areas which focus groups cannot tackle as readily as other methods – the reporting of *individual* behaviour, *individual* norms and under-standings, patterns of prevalence and incidence, changes over time, etc. So focus groups are not a quick fix and for many topics are inferior to other traditional approaches as a stand-alone method.

Nevertheless, focus groups will not dwindle into a mere historical curiosity like the Ninja Turtles or the Hula-hoop; they will continue to be used by researchers. This is partly because focus groups have become part of the mixed economy of social research, one component in multi-method research strategies, where *multiple* methods are themselves an emblem of methodological rigour. It is also partly because focus groups are demonstrably the method of choice in one narrow sub-spectrum of the broad band of sociological topic areas, namely that of the documentation of group norms and understandings. And it is partly because the possibilities of virtual focus groups have still to be fully explored and are still expanding as e-mail access is expanding; already it is clear that virtual focus groups have great advantages in economy and in participant convenience and that the electronic medium allows virtual focus groups to behave in quite different ways from 'real life' focus groups.

Our assertion of a continuing but limited role for focus groups is best substantiated by the specification of criteria for using focus groups and of ground rules for their effective operation. Kitzinger and Barbour (1999) have argued forcefully against a 'one-size-fits-all' approach to focus group methods, and in favour of a creative approach to research designs which are consonant with the particular features of the research problem at hand. This is good sense. But any purchaser of a text on focus groups would have a right to feel shortchanged if she found no suggested ground rules for their use. So we attempt this task below, emphasizing that these are suggestions and not a template. Finally, we close the book with a return to the issue of public participation in research and the question of how far focus group methods can assist in realizing effective participation.

Criteria for the use and effective deployment of focus groups

Focus groups have a less prominent role as a stand-alone method than as an ancillary method within a multi-method research design. *As a stand-alone method, focus groups only have an advantage in researching topics relating to group norms, the group meanings that underpin those norms, and the group processes whereby those meanings are constructed.* Focus groups are a particularly advantageous method where these group norms, meanings and processes are hidden or counter-cultural, but focus groups are not the best means of mapping differences in individual behaviour and behaviour change. *As an ancillary method, focus groups may be used as an initial stage of a larger study, as a means of preliminary exploration, or of the collection of everyday group language terms or the collection of group narratives, all for later use in subsequent stages of the study.* A multi-method design (which may include focus groups) will often reflect best practice, but it does not provide validation of the findings through 'triangulation'. *Instead, focus groups may be used to clarify, extend, qualify or contest findings on the same topic produced by other methods*: multiple methods cannot validate, but they can deepen our understanding of the topic. *At the end of a project, focus groups can be useful means of feeding early results back to study participants*; participants' reactions in such end-of-study groups can themselves be a useful source of data for analysis. Virtual focus groups have an additional advantage of being conductable over an extended period of weeks and even months and can therefore be can be repeatedly consulted. *Such virtual focus groups can thus be repeatedly reconvened to consider fresh results from other methods, or repeatedly consulted to derive consensual statements of group belief or policy – an electronic Delphi Group.*

Focus groups should not be controlled or directed, but they require extensive preparation and planning if they are to be successful. *The venue should always be chosen with an eye to recruitment and to minimizing the numbers of refusals and non-arrivals.* Background socio-demographic information may be available on group members as part of data from some wider study. But even if such background data are available, *it is advisable to ask participants to complete pre-group individual questionnaires to check for initial differences of opinion or behaviour within the group.* These within-group differences may sometimes be under-stated in group interaction. *It is good practice to ask each participant to introduce themselves briefly,* as an aid to voice recognition during audiotranscription. *Focusing exercises (such as ranking exercises, vignettes, the fictional 'news bulletin', or photo interpretations) will be required to focus the group's attention on the core study topic;* such exercises also make subsequent comparative analysis more straightforward. The facilitator may occasionally have to draw the attention of a wandering group back to the task in hand, but *the facilitator's main role should be to ensure all the group play a part and all viewpoints are heard.* Where an attendance allowance is provided, then the focus group may last rather longer, but in the absence of payment *two hours may be thought to be the permissible maximum length for the group meeting. At the end of each meeting there should be an opportunity for individual debriefing* of those participants who seek it or who appear distressed.

Since the main purpose of focus groups is to access group norms and understandings, *there are clear advantages in recruiting participants from pre-existing social groups.* Focus groups drawn from pre-existing social groups may also be less likely to suffer from non-attendance. However, *participant over-disclosure may be a problem* in focus groups drawn from pre-existing groups, compared to those drawn from strangers. Where pre-existing groups may contain some sub-groups who may be inhibited by others (for example, subordinates within a hierarchical workgroup), then *participants should be deliberately differentially selected from within pre-existing groups so as to maximize free discussion* (for example, in adolescent groups, boys and girls may be recruited into separate groups). The generalizability of findings needs to be assured, not by the proportionate representativeness of the participants of the various groups to the wider study population, but by *ensuring that the different groups when taken together cover the complete **range** of the study population.* Bearing in mind that a single 90-minute focus group can easily generate 100 pages of transcript, *the total number of groups recruited needs to kept to the absolute minimum consistent with covering the range of the study population.* Recruitment problems (and particularly non-arrival of participants) are arguably the greatest source of failure in focus group research and *particular attention needs to be devoted to means of ensuring maximum* *attendance; it is prudent to compensate for non-arrivals by a degree of deliberate over-recruitment.* There is no consensus on the ideal number of participants per group and this may vary by topic and by study population, but *6 to 8 individuals seems to be a good thumbnail estimate of the optimum group size;* smaller groups are said to yield greater depth of discussion, but are clearly more vulnerable to the non-arrival of participants.

Virtual focus groups have a host of advantages over conventional focus groups. They are economical (no attendance costs, no audio-transcription costs). They are not narrowly time-limited, stretching over weeks and months. They may embrace many more participants than conventional groups and participants can be highly geographically dispersed. A number of different lines of discussion may be embarked upon at the same time. And participants may prefer the convenience of being able to respond at a time and a place of their own choosing. The main disadvantage remains, of course, the relative exclusiveness of Internet use, although the demographic disparities are diminishing over time. At present, this means that *virtual focus groups are either best used in respect of a study population and of a research topic where e-mail communication would not be unusual, or they are best used alongside conventional groups.* As with any online discussion group, there will be some 'lurkers' who are not drawn into active participation in the discussion. Virtual focus groups are too recent a phenomenon for us to offer extensive guidance on how to maximize participation levels, but it is clear that *for the moderator to specify at the outset that the discussion is time-limited will ensure that at least some of the participants will make a conscious effort not to miss 'deadlines' and so increase the participation rate.*

Analysis of focus groups in commercial market research is typically based on written reports or oral debriefings of the facilitators. But *all analysis of focus groups in academic social research should be based on audio-transcription* (or the print-out of the online discussions in virtual focus groups): attempts at analysis without transcription will be prey to the dangers of selectivity and will also lose most of the richness of the data. But audiotranscription is expensive in time and money: an hour of focus group discussion is commonly said to take 8 hours to transcribe. Focus groups are not a cheap research option. A transcript is not required of the level of complexity and detail found in conversation-analytic studies (see, for example, Atkinson and Heritage, 1984), but *the transcript does need to be sufficiently faithful to convey a clear account of events*: it should record secondary as well as dominant voices, interrupted speech, false starts and hesitancies, etc. *It is good practice for the researcher to undertake the transcription of at least a few of the tapes,* in order to develop a practised grasp of the data and in order to be able to instruct the audio transcriber by example in the degree of detail required. *In order to guard against selectivity and to ensure that analysis is based on all the group discussions pertaining to a given analytical topic, it will be necessary to index the data by topic.* Note that data indexing, like book indexing, is a quite different exercise from coding: any given piece of text may be assigned to a number of different index items rather than to a single exclusive code. Where there are only a small number of transcripts (say half a dozen or so), then indexed items may be collated manually, say in a card index, *where there is a substantial amount of data to deal with it will be more convenient to use one of the qualitative data computing packages*, such as NUD•IST. Such packages are, of course, only an aid to analysis, providing an efficient system of storage and retrieval. *Analysis proceeds on a comparative basis (with a particular eye to comparisons between groups) and will be most rigorous if conducted on a stepwise basis*. Two possible systems of stepwise analysis are 'analytic induction' (Frankland and Bloor, 1999) and 'logical analysis' (Williams, 1990): the former aims to extend the analysis by attention to deviant or negative cases, while the latter searches for premises for stated beliefs and for links between them. However, it must be owned that while a systematic approach to the analysis of data is needed, the very richness of focus group data throws up unresolvable ambiguities and uncertainties which will hamstring too rigid and schematic an analytical approach. The participative character of focus group methods may stimulate a demand for the early feedback of the results of analysis to ex-group participants; this would be a valuable exercise in respect of displaying courtesy to participants, easing prior research access and disseminating findings, but it is not a means of validating findings (Bloor, 1997).

Focus groups and participatory research

Focus groups have been portrayed as a medium for democratic participation in scientific research. Rather confusingly, however, this participatory function is reported as being achieved in a number of different ways: first, it is claimed that focus groups can serve as a medium for the authentic representation of lay collective viewpoints, which can serve as a challenge to expert opinion; second, and more subtly, focus groups are more than just a forum for the representation of group views, they are a medium for the active formation for such views; third, they are more than just a medium for the formation of group views, they are a starting point for transformative collective action; and finally focus groups may be a means of lay co-participation in social science research, with co-participation in the study design, in the conduct of the study (via so-called 'indigenous researchers'), and in the consideration of the results (via a process of so-called 'extended peer review').

From their very beginnings, focus groups have of course been portrayed as a means of generating information on public understandings and viewpoints. This has been the whole basis of commercial market research using focus groups and it remains the mainspring of efforts to run groups designed to elicit clients' viewpoints across a spectrum of

public and private services. Cunningham-Burley et al. (1999) have analysed how the rise of consumerism in late modernity has assisted the
growth of focus groups as a technology which seeks to access consumers'
and users' views. They point out that, paradoxically, such research treats
focus group members as passive objects: their participation is confined to
the contribution of their views and no further participation is required of
them; criticism of the conduct of services by consumers/users is the
stimulus for remedial action by a beneficent management, not action by
the focus group members. However, alongside this consumerist approach
to focus groups, we can chart a parallel counter-cultural approach which
views the results from focus groups as an alternative and authentic
depiction of social reality which contests and confounds the previous
conventional wisdom, manifested either by expert opinion ('doctor
knows best') or by the results of 'suspect' research methods, such as
commercial opinion polls. This counter-cultural approach performs a
valuable function in reporting so-called 'silenced voices' of patients,
clients, threatened local communities, workers, ethnic minorities, and the
like. But focus groups are not The Voice of the People, any more than oral
history is The History of the Oppressed. There is a danger of viewing
focus group findings as somehow the direct, untrammelled and transparent reporting of our inner nature, an approach that Silverman (1989)
has criticized as 'the impossible dream of romanticism', referring back to
the artistic aspirations of the nineteenth-century Romantic Movement to
access directly 'true' feelings and 'real' nature.

In fact, all research methods (focus groups included) construct as well
as report their findings, the medium is part of the message. This should
not be a matter for despair, or the renunciation of empirical research in
favour of the circular deconstruction of texts (and texts-about-texts).
Rather, there is a requirement, alongside the tasks of analysis and
reportage, for the researcher to maintain a reflexive awareness of how
focus group methods actively *formulate* group norms and understandings as well as report them. This kind of reflexive approach is found, for
example, in Waterton and Wynne's (1999) report of the focus groups
they ran with community groups in West Cumbria about local reactions
to the nuclear industry at the nearby Sellafield complex. Their research
combined, on the one hand, a depiction of local concerns about nuclear
risks (which are much more complex, fluid and ambiguous than would
appear from local commercial opinion polling), with on the other hand,
an awareness of how group views unfolded and developed processually,
shaped by irony, humour and a consciousness of the presence of the
outsider/researcher.

Beyond the role of focus groups in producing contextual formulations
of group's views, it is sometimes claimed that focus groups can be a
starting point for transformative action by those groups. Having found a
voice, groups may develop an awareness of their common predicament
and attempt a collective remedy. This supposed emancipatory role for

focus group research, sometimes called Participatory Action Research (PAR), has its origins in the writings of the Brazilian educationalist, Paulo Freire, who described his group work with the poor and illiterate peasants of North-East Brazil as 'conscientization . . . the process in which men [*sic*], not as recipients, but as knowing subjects, achieve a deepening awareness of the sociocultural reality which shapes their lives and their capacity to transform that reality' (Freire, 1972, 51fn.). Adopted in kindred fields to education, such as health promotion (see, for example, the discussion in health promotion textbooks such as that of Tones et al., 1990), conscientization has become a common avowed objective of group work, focus groups included. The emancipatory claims for this approach to group work are large (so large that Freire had to leave Brazil in the days of the military junta there), but the reported emancipatory fruits of focus groups in the developed world are, to date, rather modest. Reports of transformative focus groups such as the one for carers of elderly persons in Lancashire (described by Johnson, 1996), or those for ethnic minority women under-using breast and cervical screening services in South Yorkshire (described by Chiu and Knight, 1999), all describe experiences that have been transformative for the facilitators, have involved the recognition of a common predicament among the group participants, and (in the Lancashire example) have generated collective support within the group itself and group suggestions on the redevelopment of services. However, there are no reports of this transformative activity extending in time and space beyond the focus group itself, and it is therefore unclear how far such focus groups may be emancipatory rather than merely cathartic.

Public co-participation in research through focus groups has been particularly developed in anthropological research. The guidelines for ethical practice in anthropological research issued by the professional association, the British-based Association of Social Anthropologists, require that 'as far as possible anthropologists should try and involve the people being studied in the planning and execution of research projects' (ASA, 1987: 6). There has been a longstanding view that greater local participation in Third World development projects will increase their effectiveness and it has seemed natural to extend that local participation in development projects to the research studies taking place alongside those projects (Baker and Hinton, 1999).

A project focus group is not the same as a project steering group, in the latter the group controls the execution of the project. Of course, it is perfectly possible to have research participant representation on a project steering group: Epstein's (1995) study of HIV/AIDS research and activism in the United States charts how gay activists have progressively won representation on project steering groups and on other formal bodies such as research funding councils and ethics committees. However, he also reports a process of 'expertification', whereby over time those lay representatives come increasingly to share the same viewpoint as their fellow committee members, the AIDS scientists: the scientific agenda of AIDS activist leaders has now come full circle, from that of speeding up the availability of new drug treatments, to demanding more long-term basic research. A project focus group reviews and deliberates upon the direction and conduct of the project, but it does not have direct executive control. Instead, the project executive (the grantholder(s) and researcher(s)) are required to translate, in a way that may be unclear or disputatious, the views of the focus group into everyday project decisions – general agreements still need particular applications. The project focus group becomes a standing panel, and as with Epstein's AIDS activists, there is a danger of creeping expertification, with the panelists becoming increasingly unrepresentative of their constituency. If expertification is combated by group member replacement, there may be a danger of inconsistency of viewpoints between earlier and later meetings. And whatever the success of the project focus group in dealing with its agenda, everyone who has been a contract researcher knows that not every important incident that occurs on a project gets onto agendas and into public knowledge.

This is not to say that public participation in the planning and direction of social science research is impossible, only that there may be many difficulties of execution. Certainly, there are seemingly successful examples of such public co-participation, for example, the Science Shops, originally set up in Dutch universities and now spread to many Western European countries (see the discussion in Irwin, 1995: 141–167). However, our interest here is in the more limited topic of the role of focus groups in such public co-participation. Such focus group co-participation can occur at the outset of the study, during the conduct of the study, and at the end.

Focus group involvement can occur in the design of research, but probably the most effective medium of co-participation is at a still-earlier stage of the research process, that of the selection of the topic of research itself. Focus groups can be used in order to derive a set of research priorities and indeed have been used for this purpose, with varying success, by some funding bodies. The conventional limitation of such prioritization exercises is that the topics prioritized tend to be rather general (say, the topic of community care for frail elderly people) and require a substantial further amount of specification (say, the development of a measure to evaluate the success of early hospital discharge schemes for frail elderly patients) before they can be operationalized as a research project. One way around that limitation is to provide the focus group with a ready-made list of operationalizable research projects from which to choose: the focus group will then treat the list of projects as a ranking exercise, as described in Chapter 3.

Another related possibility is currently being trialled in Cardiff by the Health and Social Care Research Support Unit there. The unit was recently set up to provide research advice and support to practitioners in the local health and social services. As well as responding to service providers' research queries, the unit aims to set up active research collaborations with local practitioners, but first it is seeking to establish what the local priorities for research should be. In order to do this, the unit has set up a virtual focus group with research-active representatives from most local agencies (health service trusts, social services departments, etc.). This virtual focus group is designed to act over time rather like an electronic Delphi Group, moving progressively and consensually to a more and more specific and operationalizable set of research topics. These operationalizable research topics can then be ranked by interviewed community representatives, such as members of community health councils, and by 'real' focus groups drawn from services users and community groups.

Baker and Hinton (1999) provide a thoughtful commentary on co-participation in the conduct of research by so-called 'indigenous' researchers in their account of two anthropological studies in Nepal. Of course, the use of so-called 'indigenous' researchers is not confined to focus group research, but indigenous focus group facilitators may play a less subordinate role in a given study project than, say, indigenous interviewers. The advantages of such public participation in focus group research are obvious: the opportunity to collect more extensive data at limited additional cost, a sense of co-ownership of the project among community members, easier recruitment of group participants, more honest responses from participants, a pre-existing familiarity with the life and culture of the researched group, and, most important of all, a shared language.

To amplify the last point, most focus groups with indigenous facilitators in the developed world are conducted among ethnic minorities. For example, many UK health authorities and NHS trusts, obliged contractually to monitor the quality of their health services provision, have attempted to supplement their patient satisfaction surveys (which may disadvantage those whose first language is not English) by focus groups conducted among ethnic minority patients by ethnic minority facilitators (see for example, Shah et al., 1993). The supposed advantages of facilitation by ethnic minority co-researchers are somewhat vitiated, however, where it proves impracticable or impossible to find a suitable facilitator for each separate ethnic group. Even when matching of facilitator and members does take place, it may be spurious: a focus group of UK health service use by Bangladeshis may be facilitated by a middle-class Bengali speaker, but most Bangladeshi patients in UK hospitals will be from the Sylheti-speaking rural north of the country. Similarly, in a series of focus groups conducted on the health beliefs of the UK Chinese population, it only proved advantageous to conduct the focus groups in Cantonese with the older age group: younger UK Chinese participants struggled with Cantonese and switched rapidly into English (Prior et al., forthcoming).

The use of focus groups as a means of co-participation at the end of the study, has already been raised in Chapter 1 in respect of the misleading notion that end-of-project feedback groups can act as a validation exercise for an earlier analysis. It was suggested that feedback groups could form a number of important functions (such as the early dissemination of findings), but validation of findings was not one of them. As we have seen, the composition and conduct of focus groups are subject to too much uncertainty, variation and frailty to permit belief in anything but highly context-dependent sets of results. However, this is not to deny the possible value to the researcher of monitoring the reactions of participants to the analysis. Rather, the results of feedback focus groups simply become another source of data to analyse. Interest in feedback groups, used since the 1970s, has been re-stimulated recently by new work in the Sociology of Scientific Knowledge, which has suggested that feedback groups can act as part of an 'extended system of peer review' (Funtowicz and Ravetz, 1993; Irwin, 1995). Just as professional scientific colleagues act as a final court of judgement on scientific findings (commenting on the adequacy of the methodology, examining possible alternative explanations, and so on), as part of their function as peer reviewers of scientific articles submitted for publication in professional journals and of end-of-grant reports to funding bodies, so also groups of lay persons, who have an understanding of the research topic through their lived experience, may also be an important source of critical appraisal. Just as professional scientific colleagues may react to findings and those reactions may lead to important modifications in the final published report, so also groups of lay persons may contribute comments which may modify and enrich that same final report. It is suggested that lay experts become part of an extended peer community of scientists, playing their part along with other experts in the interactive appraisal of research findings and acting, not as validators, but as one further potential source of analytic ideas. In broadening the peer community of scientists in this way, it is argued that the overall quality of scientific work will be improved. As evidential support for this contention, one can point to the way in which groups of workers exposed to occupational hazards have often, in the past, come to a quicker understanding of the nature of those hazards than the scientific community: 'popular epidemiology', as it is termed, may outstrip scientific epidemiology (see for example miners' early understanding of the harmful effects of excessive dust, Bloor, 2000).

Focus groups may therefore be held up as a potential tool of a new 'citizen science'. But it is important not to overstate their usefulness or understate their frailties.

References

Adler, M. and Ziglio, E. (1996) *Gazing into the Oracle: The Delphi Method and its Application to Social Policy and Public Health*. London: Jessica Kingsley.

American Sociological Association Code of Ethics (1997) www.asanet.org/ecoderev.htm

ASA (Association of Social Anthropologists) (1987) *Ethical Guidelines for Good Practice*. London: Association of Social Anthropologists.

Atkinson, J.M. and Heritage, J. (1984) *Structures of Social Action: Studies in Conversation Analysis*. Cambridge: Cambridge University Press.

Atkinson, P. (1992) *Understanding Ethnographic Texts*. London: Sage.

Babbie, E. (1992) *The Practice of Social Research*, 6th edn. Belmont, CA: Wadsworth.

Baker, R. and Hinton, R. (1999) 'Do focus groups facilitate meaningful participation in social research?', in R. Barbour and J. Kitzinger (eds) *Developing Focus Group Research: Politics, Theory and Practice*. London: Sage.

Barbour, R. (1999) 'The case for combining qualitative and quantitative approaches in health services research', *Journal of Health Services Research & Policy*, 4: 39–43.

Barbour, R. and Kitzinger, J. (eds) (1999) *Developing Focus Group Research: Politics, Theory and Practice*. London: Sage.

Basch, C.E. (1987) 'Focus group interview: an under-utilised research technique for improving theory and practice in health education', *Health Education Quarterly*, 14 (4): 411–448.

Bloor, M. (1978) 'On the analysis of observational data: a discussion of the worth and uses of inductive techniques and respondent validation', *Sociology*, 12 (3): 545–552.

Bloor, M. (1980) 'An alternative to the ethnomethodological approach to rule-use? A comment on Zimmerman and Wieder's comment on Denzin', *Scottish Journal of Sociology*, 4: 249–263. Reprinted in Bloor, M. (1997) *Selected Writings in Medical Sociological Research*. Aldershot: Ashgate.

Bloor, M. (1981) 'Therapeutic paradox: the patient culture and the formal treatment programme in a therapeutic community', *British Journal of Medical Psychology*, 54: 359–369.

Bloor, M. (1997) 'Techniques of validation in qualitative research: a critical commentary', in G. Miller and R. Dingwall (eds) *Context and Method in Qualitative Research*. London: Sage.

Bloor, M. (2000) 'The South Wales Miners Federation, Miners' Lung and the instrumental use of expertise, 1900–1950', *Social Studies of Science*, 30: 125–140.

Bloor, M., Frankland, J., Parry-Langdon, N., Robinson, M., Allerston, S., Catherine, A., Cooper, L., Gibbs, L., Gibbs, N., Hamilton-Kirkwood, L., Jones, E., Smith, W. and Spragg, B. (1999) 'A controlled evaluation of an intensive, peer-led, schools-based, anti-smoking programme', *Health Education Journal*, 58: 17–25.

Bloor, M. and McIntosh, J. (1989) 'Power, surveillance and resistance: a comparison of reactions to surveillance in therapeutic communities and health visiting', in S. Cunningham-Burley and N. McKeganey (eds) *Readings in Medical Sociology*. London: Tavistock.

Bloor, M., McKeganey, N. and Fonkert, D. (1988) *One Foot in Eden: A Sociological Study of the Range of Therapeutic Community Practice*. London: Routledge.

Bourdieu, P. (1977) *Outline of a Theory of Practice*. Cambridge: Cambridge University Press.

Branestorm (1998) www.branestorm.com/conference/facts.htm

Bulmer, M. (1982) *The Uses of Social Research*. London: Allen and Unwin.

Bulmer, M. (1984) 'Concepts in the analysis of qualitative data', in M. Bulmer (ed.) *Sociological Research Methods: An Introduction*. London: Macmillan.

Carey, J. (1975) *Sociology and Public Affairs: the Chicago School*. London: Sage.

Catterall, M. and Maclaran, P. (1997) 'Focus group data and qualitative analysis', *Sociological Research Online*, 2, 1. http://www.socresonline.org.uk/socresonline/2/1/6.html

Chiu, L.F. and Knight, D. (1999) 'How useful are focus groups in obtaining the views of minority groups?', in R.S. Barbour and J. Kitzinger (eds) *Developing Focus Group Research: Politics, Theory and Practice*. London: Sage.

Coffey, A. and Atkinson, P. (1996) *Making Sense of Qualitative Data*. London: Sage.

Collins, H.M. (1981) 'The place of the "core-set" in modern science: social contingency with methodological propriety in science', *History of Science*, 19: 6–19.

Coomber, R. (1997) 'Using the Internet for survey research', *Sociological Research Online*, 2, 2.

Coulter, J. (1974) 'The ethnomethodological programme in contemporary sociology', *The Human Context*, 6: 103–122.

Cressey, D.R. (1953) *Other Peoples' Money: A Study of the Social Psychology of Embezzlement*. New York: Free Press.

Cunningham-Burley, S., Kerr, A. and Pavis, S. (1999) 'Theorizing subjects and subject matter in focus group research', in R. Barbour and J. Kitzinger (eds) *Developing Focus Group Research: Politics, Theory and Practice*. London: Sage.

Denzin, N. (1989) *The Research Act: A Theoretical Introduction to Sociological Methods*. Englewood Cliffs, NJ: Prentice-Hall (first edition 1970).

Dey, I. (1993) *Qualitative Data Analysis: A User-Friendly Guide for Social Scientists*. London: Routledge.

Diamond, A. and Goddard, E. (1995) *Smoking among Secondary School Children in 1994*. London: HMSO.

Douglas, J.D. (1976) *Investigative Social Research: Individual and Team Field Research*. Beverly Hills, CA: Sage.

Duncombe, J. and Marsden, D. (1996) 'Can we research the private sphere? methodological and ethical problems in the study of the role of intimate emotion in personal relationships', in L. Morris and E. Stina Lyon (eds) *Gender Relations in Public and in Private: New Research Perspectives*. Explorations in Sociology 43, British Sociological Association, London: Macmillan.

Elgesem, D. (1996) 'Privacy, respect for persons and risk', in C. Ess (ed.) *Philosophical Perspectives on Computer-Mediated Communication*. Albany: State University of New York Press.

Emerson, R. (1981) 'Observational fieldwork', *Annual Review of Sociology*, 7: 351–378.

Emerson, R.M. and Pollner, M. (1988) 'On the uses of members' responses to researchers' accounts', *Human Organization*, 47: 189–198.

Epstein, S. (1995) *Impure Science: AIDS Activism and the Politics of Knowledge*. Berkeley: University of California Press.

Farquhar, C. and Das, R. (1999) 'Are focus groups suitable for "sensitive" topics?', in R. Barbour and J. Kitzinger (eds) *Developing Focus Group Research: Politics, Theory and Practice*. London: Sage.

Finch, J. (1984) '"It's great to have someone to talk to": the ethics and politics of interviewing women', in C. Bell and H. Roberts (eds) *Social Researching: Politics, Problems and Practice*. London: Routledge.

Foucault, M. (1980) 'The eye of power', in C. Gordon (ed.) *M. Foucault Power/Knowledge*. London: Harvester.

Frankland, J. and Bloor, M. (1999) 'Some issues arising in the systematic analysis of focus group materials', in R. Barbour and J. Kitzinger (eds) *Developing Focus Group Research*. London: Sage.

Freire, P. (1972) *Cultural Action for Freedom*. Harmondsworth: Penguin.

Funtowicz, S.O. and Ravetz, J. (1993) 'Science for the post-normal age', *Futures*, 25: 739–755.

Garfinkel, H. (1967) *Studies in Ethnomethodology*. Englewood Cliffs, NJ: Prentice-Hall.

Giddens, A. (1991) *Modernity and Self-Identity: Self and Society in the Late Modern Age*. Cambridge: Polity.

Green, J. and Hart, L. (1999) 'The impact of context on data', in R. Barbour and J. Kitzinger (eds) *Developing Focus Group Research: Politics, Theory and Practice*. London: Sage.

Greenbaum, T. (1998) *The Handbook for Focus Group Research*, 2nd edn. Thousand Oaks: Sage.

Griffin, C. (1986) 'Qualitative methods and female experience: young women from school to the job market', in S. Wilkinson (ed.) *Feminist Social Psychology: Developing Theory and Practice*. Milton Keynes: Open University Press.

Hammersley, M. (1989) *The Dilemma of Qualitative Method: Herbert Blumer and the Chicago Tradition*. London: Routledge.

Hammersley, M. (1995) *The Politics of Social Research*. London: Sage.

Hammersley, M. and Atkinson, P. (1995) *Ethnography: Principles in Practice*. London: Sage.

Hey, V. (1997) *The Company She Keeps: An Ethnography of Girls' Friendship*. Buckingham, PA: Open University Press.

Hodder, I. (1994) 'The interpretation of documents and material culture', in N.K. Denzin and Y.S. Lincoln (eds) *Handbook of Qualitative Research*. Thousand Oaks: Sage.

Holstein, J. and Gubrium, J. (1995) *The Active Interview*. Thousand Oaks: Sage.

Hughes, R. (1998) 'Considering the vignette technique and its application to a study of doing injecting and HIV risk and safer behaviour', *Sociology of Health & Illness*, 20: 381–400.

Irwin, A. (1995) *Citizen Science: A Study of People, Expertise and Sustainable Development*. London: Routledge.

Jasanoff, S. (1990) *The Fifth Branch: Science Advisors as Policymakers*. Cambridge, MA: Harvard University Press.

Jasanoff, S. (1995) *Science at the Bar*. Cambridge, MA: Harvard University Press.

Johnson, A. (1996) 'It's good to talk: the focus group and the sociological imagination', *The Sociological Review*, 44: 517–538.

Kendall, L. (1999) 'Recontextualising "cyberspace": methodological considerations for online research', in S. Jones (ed.) *Doing Internet Research*. Newbury Park: Sage.

Khan, M.E. and Manderson, L. (1992) 'Focus groups in tropic diseases research', *Health Policy and Planning*, 7: 56–66.

Kitzinger, J. (1993) 'Understanding AIDS: researching audience perceptions of acquired immune deficiency syndrome', in J. Eldridge (ed.) *Getting the Message*. London: Routledge.

Kitzinger, J. (1994a) 'Focus groups: method or madness?', in M. Boulton (ed.) *Challenge and Innovation: Methodological Advances in Social Research on HIV/AIDS*. London: Taylor and Francis.

Kitzinger, J. (1994b) 'The methodology of focus groups: the importance of interaction between research participants', *Sociology of Health & Illness*, 16 (1): 103–121.

Kitzinger, J. and Barbour, R. (1999) 'Introduction: the challenge and promise of focus groups', in R. Barbour and J. Kitzinger (eds) *Developing Focus Group Research: Politics, Theory and Practice*. London: Sage.

Kitzinger, J. and Farquar, C. (1999) 'The analytic potential of "sensitive moments" in focus group discussions', in R. Barbour and J. Kitzinger (eds) *Developing Focus Group Research: Politics, Theory and Practice*. London: Sage

Krueger, R.A. (1994) *Focus Groups: a Practical Guide for Applied Research*, 2nd edn. Thousand Oaks: Sage.

Krueger, R.A. (1995) 'The future of focus groups', *Qualitative Health Research*, 5 (4): 524–530.

Krueger, R.A. (1998) *Moderating Focus Groups*. Thousand Oaks: Sage.

Langford, D. (1995a) *Practical Computer Ethics*. Maidenhead: McGraw Hill.

Langford, D. (1995b) 'Law and disorder in Netville', *New Scientist*, 146: 52–53.

Lindesmith, A.L. (1947) *Opiate Addiction*. Bloomington, IN: Principia Press.

Lofland, J. and Lofland, L.H. (1995) *Analyzing Social Settings. A Guide to Qualitative Observation and Analysis*. London: Wadsworth.

Madriz, E.I. (1998) 'Using focus groups with lower socioeconomic status Latina women', *Qualitative Inquiry*, 4 (1): 114–128.

Maxwell, C. and Boyle, M. (1995) 'Risky heterosexual practices amongst women over 30: gender, power and long-term relationships', *AIDS Care*, 7 (3): 277–293.

Mays, V., Cochrane, S. and Bellinger, G. (1992) 'The language of black gay men's sexual behaviour: implications for AIDS risk reduction', *Journal of Sex Research*, 29: 425–434.

McKeganey, N. (1995) 'Quantitative and qualitative research in the addictions: an unhelpful divide', *Addiction*, 90: 749–51.

McRobbie, A. and Garber, J. (1976) 'Girls and subcultures: an exploration', in S. Hall and T. Jefferson (eds) *Resistance through Ritual*. London: Hutchinson.

Merton, R. (1987) 'Focused interviews and focus groups: continuities and discontinuities', *Public Opinion Quarterly*, 51: 550–557.

Merton, R. and Kendall, P. (1946) 'The focused interview', *American Journal of Sociology*, 51: 541–557.

Merton, R., Fiske, M. and Kendall, P. (1990) *The Focused Interview*. Glencoe: The Free Press (original edition 1956).

Michell, L. (1999) 'Combining focus groups and interviews: telling how it is; telling how it feels', in R. Barbour and J. Kitzinger (eds) *Developing Focus Group Research: Politics, Theory and Practice*. London: Sage.

Michell, L. and Amos, A. (1997) 'Girls, pecking order and smoking', *Social Science and Medicine*, 44 (12): 1861–1869.

Middleton, S., Ashworth, K. and Walker, R. (1994) *Small Fortunes: Pressures on Parents and Children in the 1990s*. London: CPAG.

Miles, M.B. and Huberman, A.M. (1994) *Qualitative Data Analysis. An Expanded Sourcebook*. London: Sage.

Morgan, D. (1988) *Focus Groups as Qualitative Research*. Newbury Park: Sage.

Morgan, D. (1992) 'Designing focus group research', in M. Stewart et al. (eds) *Tools for Primary Care Research Volume 2*. London: Sage.

Morgan, D. (1995) 'Why things (sometimes) go wrong in focus groups', *Qualitative Health Research*, 5 (4): 516–523.

Morgan, D. (1997) *Focus Groups as Qualitative Research*, 2nd edn. Thousand Oaks: Sage.

Morgan, D.L. (1998) *The Focus Group Guidebook*. Thousand Oaks: Sage.

Morgan, D.L. and Krueger, R.A. (1993) 'When to use focus groups and why', in D.L. Morgan (ed.) *Successful Focus Groups: Advancing the State of the Art*. Thousand Oaks: Sage.

Morgan, D.L. and Spanish, M. (1984) 'Focus groups: a new tool for qualitative research', *Qualitative Sociology*, 7: 253–270.

Murray, P. (1997). 'Using virtual focus groups in qualitative research', *Qualitative Health Research*, 7 (4): 542–549.

Myers, G. (1998) 'Displaying opinions: topics and disagreement in focus groups', *Language in Society*, 27: 85–111.

Myers, G. and Macnaghten, P. (1999) 'Can focus groups be analysed as talk?', in R. Barbour and J. Kitzinger (eds) *Developing Focus Group Research: Politics, Theory and Practice*. London: Sage.

Nix, L.M., Pasteur, A.B. and Servance, M.A. (1988) 'A focus group study of sexually active black male teenagers', *Adolescence*, XXII (91).

Oakley, A. (1981) 'Interviewing women: a contradiction in terms', in H. Roberts (ed.) *Doing Feminist Research*. London: Routledge.

Philo, G. (1990) *Seeing and Believing*. London: Routledge.

Pugsley, L. (1996) 'Focus groups, young people and sex education', in J. Pilcher and A. Coffey (eds) *Gender and Qualitative Research*. Aldershot: Avebury.

Prior, L., Pang, L.C. and See, B.H. (forthcoming) 'Lay beliefs, lay knowledge and lay expertise: a study with Chinese characters', *Sociology of Health & Illness*.

Quine, S. and Cameron, I. (1995) 'The use of focus groups with disabled elderly', *Qualitative Health Research*, 5 (4): 454–462.

Reid, M. (1983) 'A feminist sociological imagination? reading Ann Oakley', *Sociology of Health & Illness*, 5: 83–94.

Richards, T.J. and Richards, L. (1994) 'Using computers in qualitative research', in N.K. Denzin and Y.S. Lincoln (eds) *Handbook of Qualitative Research*. London: Sage.

Robinson, W.S. (1951) 'The logical structure of analytic induction', *American Sociological Review*, 16: 812–818.

Robson, K. (1999) Perceptions of oral health care services in Bro Taf. Unpublished report for Bro Taf Health Authority.

Robson, K. (2000) 'Lay evaluations of quality of care and skill', paper presented at the International and American Association for Dental Research Annual Meeting, Washington DC, 5–8 April.

Robson, K. and Robson, M. (1999) 'Your place or mine? ethics, the researcher and the Internet', in J. Armitage and J. Roberts (eds) *Exploring Cybersociety: Social, Political, Economic and Cultural Issues (Volume II)*. Newcastle: University of Northumbria.

Schmidt, W. (1997) 'World-wide web survey research: benefits, potential problems and solutions', *Behaviour Research Methods, Instruments and Computers*, 29, 274–279.

Schutz, A. (1962) 'Commonsense and scientific interpretation of human action', in A. Schutz *Collected Papers Volume I*. The Hague: Nijhoff.

Schutz, A. (1964a) 'The social world and the theory of social action', in A. Schutz *Collected Papers Volume II*. The Hague: Nijhoff.

Schutz, A. (1964b) 'The homecoming', in A. Schutz *Collected Papers Volume II*. The Hague: Nijhoff.

Schutz, A. (1964c) 'The well-informed citizen', in A. Schutz *Collected Papers Volume II*. The Hague: Nijhoff.

Schutz, A. (1970) *Reflections on the Problem of Relevance* (ed. R. Zaner). New Haven, CT: Yale University Press.

Schutz, A. and Luckmann, T. (1974) *The Structure of The Lifeworld*. London: Heinemann.

Seale, C. (1999) *The Quality of Qualitative Research*. London: Sage.

Selwyn, N. and Robson, K. (1998) 'Using email as a research tool', *Social Research Update*, 21. http://www.soc.surrey.ac.uk/sru/sru21.html

Shah, L., Harvey, I. and Coyle, E. (1993) *The Health and Social Care Needs of Ethnic Minorities in South Glamorgan. Phase I: A Qualitative Study*. University of Wales College of Medicine: Centre for Applied Public Health Medicine.

Sharf, B. (1999) 'Beyond netiquette: the ethics of doing naturalistic discourse research on the Internet', in S. Jones (ed.) *Doing Internet Research*. Thousand Oaks: Sage.

Silverman, D. (1989) 'Beyond enlightenment: the impossible dreams of reformism and romanticism', in D. Silverman and J. Gubrium (eds) *The Politics of Field Research: Beyond Enlightenment*. London: Sage.

Silverman, D. (1993) *Interpreting Qualitative Data: Methods of Analysing, Talk, Text and Interaction*. London: Sage.

Smith, H.W. (1995) 'Ethics in focus groups: a few concerns', *Qualitative Health Research*, 5 (4): 476–486.

Stewart, D.W. and Shamdasani, P.N. (1990) *Focus Groups: Theory and Practice*. Thousand Oaks: Sage.

Stewart, F., Eckermann, E. and Zhou, K. (1998) 'Using the Internet in qualitative public health research: a comparison of Chinese and Australian young women's perceptions of tobacco use', *Internet Journal of Health Promotion*. http://www.monash.edu.au/health/IJHP/1998/12

Stone, A.R. (1995) 'Sex and death among the disembodied: VR, cyberspace and the nature of academic discourse', in S.L. Star (ed.) *The Cultures of Computing*. Oxford: Blackwell.

Sutherland, E.H. and Cressey, D.R. (1960) *Principles of Criminology*. New York: J.B. Lippincott Company.

Sveilich, C. (1995) 'Support on the information highway', *I.B.Details*, 3 (2): 2–3.

Thomas, M. (1999) 'Foreign Affaires: A Sociological Exploration of Holiday Romance'. PhD Thesis, Cardiff University.

Thompson, S. (1998) 'Paying respondents and informants', *Social Research Update*, 14. http://www.soc.surrey.ac.uk/sru/SRU14.html

Tones, K., Tilford, S. and Robinson, Y. (1990) *Health Education: Effectiveness and Efficiency*. London: Chapman & Hall.

Tudor Hart, J. (1999) 'Going for Gold'. Pontypridd: the Welsh Institute of Health & Social Care Research, University of Glamorgan.

Vaughn, S., Shay Schumm, J. and Sinagub, J. (1996) *Focus Group Interviews in Psychology and Education*. Thousand Oaks: Sage.

Waterton, C. and Wynne, B. (1999) 'Can focus groups access community views?', in R. Barbour and J. Kitzinger (eds) *Developing Focus Group Research: Politics, Theory and Practice*. London: Sage.

Wellings, K., Field, J., Johnson, A. and Wadsworth, J. (1994) *Sexual Behaviour in Britain: The National Survey of Sexual Attitudes and Lifestyles*. Harmondsworth: Penguin.

West, P. (1982) 'Reproducing naturally occurring stories: vignettes in survey research'. Working Paper. Aberdeen: MRC Medical Sociology Unit.

White, G.E. and Thomson, A.N. (1995) 'Anonymised focus groups as a research tool for health professionals', *Qualitative Health Research*, 5 (2): 256–261.

Wilkinson, C. (1998) 'Focus groups in feminist research: power interaction, and the co-construction of meaning', *Women's Studies International Forum*, 21 (1): 111–125.

Wilkinson, C. (1999) 'How useful are focus groups in feminist research?', in R. Barbour and J. Kitzinger (eds) *Developing Focus Group Research: Politics, Theory and Practice*. London: Sage.

Williams, R.G.A. (1981a) 'Logical analysis as a qualitative method I: themes in old age and chronic illness', *Sociology of Health & Illness*, 3 (2): 140–163.

Williams, R.G.A. (1981b) 'Logical analysis as a qualitative method II: conflict of ideas and the topic of illness', *Sociology of Health & Illness*, 3 (2): 165–187.

Williams, R.G.A. (1990) *A Protestant Legacy: Attitudes to Death and Illness among Older Aberdonians*. Oxford: Clarendon Press.

Witmer, D.F., Colman, R.W. and Katzman, S.L. (1999) 'From paper-and-pencil to screen-and-keyboard: towards a methodology for survey research on the Internet', in S. Jones (ed.) *Doing Internet Research*. Thousand Oaks: Sage.

Wynne, B. (1996) 'Misunderstood misunderstandings: social identities and public uptake of science', in A. Irwin and B. Wynne (eds) *Misunderstanding Science? The Public Reconstruction of Science and Technology*. Cambridge: Cambridge University Press.

Young, J. (1994) 'Textuality in cyberspace: MUDs and written experience'. www.ludd.luth.se/mud/aber/articles/writtenexperience.thesis.html

Zimmerman, D. and Wieder, L. (1971) 'Ethnomethodology and the problem of order: comment on Denzin', in J.D. Douglas (ed.) *Understanding Everyday Life*. London: Routledge and Kegan Paul.

Znaniecki, F. (1968) *The Method of Sociology*. New York: Octagon (original edition 1934).

Index